RADICAL:
An American's Plan
For REAL Change

RADICAL:
AN AMERICAN'S PLAN
FOR REAL CHANGE

JOSHUA R. YATES

NMD Press

Library of Congress Cataloging-in-Publishing Data available upon request.
ISBN-13: 978-0615738642
ISBN-10: 0615738648

NMD Press books are available at special discounts when purchased
in bulk for premium and sales promotions as well as for fundraising or
educational use. Special editions or book excerpts can also be created to
specification. For details, contact NMD Press by sending an email to
lmyates@yatesmidwest.com.

First printing December 2012

Contents

Introduction

To The Reader:

This book is the product of many years spent talking with ordinary Americans about many key issues affecting our country. And often, in those discussions, these Americans wondered if there were any solutions to the issues affecting *them*. In these pages, I present the solutions needed to create the change we need.

I know that solving these most pressing problems may be difficult, and some of the solutions I propose you may disagree with (or you may have a different idea or approach). That is fantastic! I don't expect that everyone will agree with me on everything. All I ask is for you to keep an open mind as you read this book. I also ask that you, as an American, think of how *you* can implement some of the solutions I present to you.

After you read through these ideas and solutions, I ask that you also pass these ideas along to your elected officials, representatives, friends, and family. If we all stand together, advocating for real change with real, viable solutions, things WILL change.

I welcome your thoughts, questions, and discussion on these solutions and ideas. I also welcome any other thoughts you might have on how to move our country forward. Please visit my website at *www.newmanifestdestiny.com*, and please feel free to contact me directly anytime.

Yours,

Joshua R. Yates

Joshua R. Yates

Educational Reform

It's not uncommon, at least amongst my family, to have dinner table discussions on the issues with the current state of education in the United States. Go shopping at a store and the cashier cannot determine what the change is on a bill of $17.35 when you hand them $20 (which is $2.65 by the way), read a paper written by a third-year college student only to find "chat speak" laced through the paper, or worse, they do not understand that a paper has three parts: the introduction, the body, and the conclusion. At my first employer, I had to be able to make change without a calculator or a computer to do it for me, and prove that I could do so before I could even work with real money serving actual customers. As for writing, I remember all of the tedious assignments on grammar, spelling, and proper sentence, paragraph, and paper construction in classes prior to ever attending college. How are these not being learned by today's students?

While I was a graduate student in economics, I was tasked with the writing section of a course in United States economic history. Most of my time in office hours, when I commonly saw students whose papers I had marked to revise and resubmit due to too many errors, was spent going through basic sentence structure, grammar, spelling corrections, and in some cases, how to properly structure and write an essay. I was stunned that these students, all juniors and seniors in college, had made it this far without being able to complete a basic essay assignment, given that they all had to take two composition courses through the English department.

At the time, I was the chief steward of the graduate (student) employees' union, and determined to find out just what the issue was. After asking several graduate teaching assistants who taught composition, their response was telling. They saw the same issues repeatedly from incoming students – unfamiliarity with proper grammar, complete reliance and trust in spell checkers (which check for spelling only, not context - a common error students who rely on spell checkers make), and lack of knowledge on essay, paragraph, or sentence structure. The same students also seem to be unable to express their thoughts in an essay at all. Sadly, it is some of these same students who sit in their classes and text their friends during the lectures.

The solution to these education sector-wide issues cannot come only at the college level. They must come earlier. Students who cannot write a basic paragraph or essay, for example, should not be in college to begin with. They should have learned these skills before they attend college, if they attend at all. This is not to say there are not issues at the college (also called the post-secondary) level, they do exist and they must be dealt with in their own, separate, way. Low-paid faculty members are responsible for teaching large (almost overwhelming) course loads (with large numbers of students). These problems are pervasive, and the solutions need to cover all levels of our current educational systems.

Joshua R. Yates

Elementary and Secondary Schools

Curriculum Change and a New Educational Focus

Any changes in education curriculum usually take several years to produce measurable results and require a continual and concerted effort to succeed. If we want to change the way that colleges train the next generation of scholars, then we need to provide these colleges with better-prepared incoming students. The change needs to begin at the elementary level.

Elementary schools should provide an environment where young students can learn the most basic skills needed to prepare them for life ahead. Students at this stage should truly be focusing on learning to read, learning to write, learning basic mathematics, studying American and world history, and exploring science. Aside from these, there should be some sort of physical education, as it is important to learn how to properly exercise. Lastly, recess is critical as well. Especially in these early years, recess is a chance to socialize with peers, a chance to freely exercise, and a time when children can be wholly creative or imaginative. For example, imagining that they are a character in a movie or a show and the equipment on the playground mimics it. In my own case, it was imagining that the swings on the playground were actually jet aircraft and that my friends and I were fighter pilots shooting down enemy aircraft. It was simply a creative expression, and a way to release energy before going to back inside and getting back to work.

Rote memorization should be the major point at this level of study since all of the subject matter learned here will be used later in the child's education. You cannot do calculus or algebra if you do not understand basic arithmetic. There must be a time for creative expression, and should be encouraged. Science fairs and book writing competitions, for example, provide an outlet for creative expression and allow students to showcase their grasp and mastery of course concepts that they have been working to apply to memory. These types of activities should be encouraged, especially the finding of creative solutions to problems encountered in course material.

Secondary education, or the junior high/middle school and high school levels is where students should begin moving beyond straight rote memorization and begin looking at creativity and application of skills already learned as well as expansion of their basic skill set. This does not mean that the focus on memorization should stop. It shouldn't. These new skills are just as important to memorize. By the time the student is in the 11th or 12th grades, their coursework should rely mainly on application and extensions of knowledge already applied to memory, focusing on preparation along their intended career path. They should be preparing to make the transition either to the workforce, the military (or some other form of government service, such as a police officer or firefighter, for example), vocational school and apprenticing for a trade, or to attend a traditional college. The focus needs to be on knowledge and information acquisition in line with the student's overall goals. If they have no intention of proceeding to a traditional college and intend after graduation to enroll in a trade school or to apprentice to learn to become an electrician, as an example, then their coursework should reflect that preference. These decisions should be made to provide a guide to the individual student's course of study, at around the 10th grade. The student, an advisor, and their parents would all need to be involved.

Suppose that the student, in this case, does prefer to learn a trade rather than attend a traditional college. By allowing them to start learning the basics of their trade during the last two years of high school, functioning essentially as a junior apprentice, they will be better prepared once they graduate and to finish out their training either through a technical school or by continuing in their apprenticeship. Furthermore, for those learning a trade or simply preparing for the workforce directly, their on-the-job training or apprenticeship work would be counted, in conjunction with their employer/master (in the case of apprentices), for credit toward graduation. This allows the school to ensure that the student is being properly trained and prepared while also ensuring that the student is learning their job skills or trade as intended.

Provided that the student has taken (and passed) the requisite courses in American history, government, and culture, as well as additional courses in, say, personal finance and budgeting, basic economics, geography, English and writing, and basic mathematics, there is no reason that the student should not be allowed to graduate and move forward with their chosen path. Obviously the course selection would differ greatly from one student to the next based on their intended career path, but this diversity is strength in terms of allowing individuals to focus themselves on one path (rather than being generalists in several). In economics, this is called division of labor. If we all know how to do every step of the process, then we are less efficient and less effective than if we focused on doing one thing, doing it very well, to the exclusion of other areas of training or study. This is clearly evident when someone finishes their Ph.D., given that they are focusing in on one very particular sub field (and even then, one very specific topic within that sub field, with respect to the completion of their dissertation). However, there is no reason not to expand this to all levels of society. We once did have, and supported, division of labor on a massive scale. It was this idea that drove our nation during its industrial era. Sadly, we seem to have lost this drive with the push toward ensuring broad-based, minimal depth, liberal arts education at all levels of the educational system.

Worse still is the idea of educating students only to pass a given exam. Standardized testing does not ensure that students can handle tasks not on the exam and does a gross disservice to both the student and the educator. It runs contrary to the very essence of a division of labor. If everyone knows the same information, equally well (generally) then there are no specialists, and thus, no division of labor, resulting in poor performance in the job, lack of specialty knowledge on the job, and overall a lack of efficiency.

Making the change to an education system based around student choice and division of labor allows for our educational system to be better geared toward preparing the individual student for the path they have selected, rather than reinforcing the view that all students intend to attend a traditional college, (which is not the case, and should not be the case, for all students). Some students desire to go to college, others don't. Some have no business being in college at all. It is up to the individual to determine which path they desire, not for the system to determine for them which path they will take. If a student is not up to the task they have selected, then the system should be helping to guide them to a path that better suits their interests and abilities. That said, don't take that statement to mean I endorse school-driven choice. No, it is an affirmation – that schools should be helping students to explore options other than college for their futures.

If a student whose academic performance has been consistently poor intends to attend a traditional college, then they will need to show they have the aptitude for such study by markedly improving their performance. Furthermore, it might be best for the student to prove they are up to the challenge by taking some courses at the community college as part of their curriculum, essentially beginning the college preparation path. If they are unable to handle the rigor of the courses at the community college, then the student should be presented, through their educators, with the opportunity to alter their path and continue forward in a new one. This should be limited, so as to prevent this becoming cyclical for students. Path corrections would be allowed once, perhaps twice, but always with the knowledge that changes to their educational path in high school may result in more time spent training after or preparing after high school for either college or their chosen trade. It should be the task of our schools to help fulfill the goals and dreams of the students to the best of their ability, not to force upon them a path that is unsuited for their natural abilities.

Administrative Reform

To properly reform elementary and secondary schools, beyond curricular changes discussed earlier, we must change the institution itself. This means stronger principals, better teachers, and better compensation. It means a more efficient organization, technological upgrades, and newer facilities. It means bringing teacher unions to the table as an active participant in the discussion, beyond pay and seniority, beyond job security issues only. Unions should not be strictly shields for their workers, for better or worse. Having been a union member myself, and a union steward, the strength of any labor union is not in "what they can get for their workers" but rather the degree to which they are included in the discussion as a whole. Does the union have a seat at the table when it comes to institutional planning and determination of strategic goals? Does their influence extend to suggestions to improve the institution as a whole, from curriculum to facilities to determination of metrics to measure student progress? If they do not, then the union as a whole is not doing all that it can to serve the overall interests of its members.

Confrontation is not always the best means of achieving the overall goals of the labor union's members, and it is possible to lose a battle but still win the war. If you approach every battle as a zero-sum, no holds barred, battle royal then you will certainly lose the war, even if it is a slow death by a thousand cuts.

Unions have earned the reputation they currently have through these sorts of tactics, and they do a disservice to what collective bargaining is and should be. Membership is not simply to boost compensation as a group, protect seniority "rights," or prevent dismissals from employment. If it is, then it is a poor excuse for a labor union, and one that does not deserve a seat at the table. Instead, membership MUST be more than pursuit of the pocketbook. It must be a lifestyle, a professional choice, a statement of our values and desire to improve the strength of our collective voice through collective bargaining and collective representation. The leadership must come from the members, and must be more than just about money.

Principals and teachers must reassert their control over both their schools and their classrooms. In this capacity, both principals and teachers should consult local parents' groups for input and feedback on the school as a whole, while still acknowledging their own training and experience in serving the needs and desires of both the community (through the parents) and the students themselves. Gone, in many schools, are the days where being sent to the principal's office was actually a threat, where you dreaded the walk down the hall and where the principal was intimidating. Sure, there are some cases where this might still apply, but in general this is the anomaly now, more than the norm. If principals cannot assert control, they are relegated to being strictly an administrative bureaucrat, rather than a true headmaster. The same applies for teachers with respect to their individual classrooms. There is a trend among students (and parents) to second-guess the teacher, and to assume that if they get a poor grade that they will just have their parents call in and complain about "Teacher X" who will then let up and grade their child "easier." This is a huge disservice to the students, an ethical failure on the part of parents, and an insult to the competence of our teachers. Couple this with issues of grade inflation, teaching to standardized tests, and continual demands regarding exam performance by students being tied to continued employment (for teachers) and the result becomes an exceedingly high number of stressors on teachers and principals, and a high turnover rate among new teachers.

Furthermore, teachers (oddly enough) are being expected to teach children who increasingly disrespect them, and yet are compensated with declining benefits, uncertain employment conditions, and continual poor wages. If we expect for our teachers to be of the highest quality, then we must compensate them at a level to do so. This means that we must pay not according to years of service entirely, but also according to merit. The number of years you "survived" a classroom should not be the determining factor on what your pay is. Should there be a floor? Certainly, and that floor can be increased, tied to increase by some percentage rate above inflation or cost of living. This ensures that regardless, everyone at least maintains their current wages, rather than taking a real wage cut.

Couple these issues with merit-based increases that encourage teachers to strive to go beyond the baseline. In return, they are compensated for their efforts. This would be very similar to many compensation schemes that are utilized within other employment spheres, and could easily be duplicated to elementary and secondary education with little trouble. Sure, individuals can just stay at the baseline (and there should be no penalty for that), but if they want to achieve the higher compensation of some of their colleagues, they will need to take their teaching, and career, to a higher level. It adds a real reward for excellence without a penalty for remaining in the median.

At the same time, teachers who are not performing consistently at the median must be subject to penalty, including dismissal. We need our best to strive to become teachers, rather than retaining those who should not be teaching at all. Background checks and the like are not good predictors of teaching excellence, nor are transcripts and grades. Only observation of specific metrics (such as student knowledge retention or assessment performance) taken while the educator is on the job can provide the kind of information needed to make this sort of call. However, if you place a particular teacher into a situation that they are not suited to handle, based on their background education and experience, and then expect them to excel without the tools needed, is a recipe for disaster.

These sorts of situations must be avoided to have an honest assessment, and this reinforces the need for stronger principals. Teachers must know that their principal is their advocate and will defend them, given that all principals were once, themselves, teachers. Some may still step into the classroom if the district is small enough to necessitate it. Students must also know that, while fair, the principal is no pushover – and will wield the tools at their disposal as needed to enforce school rules, proper decorum, and to protect their teachers from abuse by students.

Efficiency of the organization ties in directly with technological upgrades and newer facilities. By newer, I do not necessarily mean wholly new buildings. Instead, I am referencing upgrades and remodeling of current buildings, as well as actually doing the needed maintenance on time. Leaks in the roof leading to buckets placed throughout the building are unacceptable. The amount of taxes paid to school districts from local property taxes requires that the organization improve efficiency, and this starts with streamlined administration and staff.

As with any educational institution, the amount of administrative overhead must not dominate the budgetary expenditures. After all, the purpose of the organization is to educate students, not to pay for fancy buildings and multitudes of redundant and/or underutilized staff. Funds should pay for appropriate buildings, necessary upgrades and remodeling, timely maintenance (preventative is best as it is ALWAYS less costly), appropriate numbers of quality faculty, and sufficient administration that can do the job (without being bloated in terms of number). Performance audits of administrative staff, periodically, will identify positions that are being underutilized, allowing for reallocation of workloads to ensure all employees are being properly tasked.

Given the digital nature of our society, and the increasing movement to all things digital, there is no reason why much of the work done by the district cannot also be done digitally. This applies in districts of any size, but will require that the district be proactive on its use of technology funds to ensure that it has the capability to operate digitally, provided that this improves efficiency. If moving digital actually slows employees down then the district has failed to adequately train their employees on the use of the software, or purchased software that was either inappropriate or overly complex for their local needs.

Why vouchers are not the solution

There has been a growing movement for some time to offer vouchers as an option for individuals who wish to send their children to private schools, rather than to the public schools. Scholars and professionals alike have opined about how the public school system is a failure – and rather than making the attempt to reform it, instead are attempting to depart from it entirely (but still want the taxpayers to pay for it). This is the wrong approach entirely. Having attended both public and private schools during my own elementary and secondary school years, simply departing the public school system for a private school does not fix anything. Both have their own problems, and flooding private schools with students will only shift the problem around, rather than resolving anything.

The only true reform our public school systems, nationwide, can hope to achieve is the kind of lasting change that many of us want to see – the sort of national shift that is needed to bring our nation to the forefront again and provide hope for a whole new generation of Americans who feel less proud to be American than many of us were at their ages.

Aside from the institutional and curricular changes noted earlier, there is a societal change that we need for our public schools, and this gets to the heart of the voucher debate. What we need, as a society, is a return to neighborhood schools. The goal should not be to ensure that each school has some set, arbitrary breakdown of individuals based on ethnicity, gender, or some other criterion. The goal must be to ensure that each neighborhood has its own schools, that it can rally around, that provide quality education for all of the children in that neighborhood, where families, children, and friends can congregate for evening activities, school sporting events, and to celebrate the accomplishments and successes of the students in that neighborhood. There is no reason why we should be bussing students across town, or between towns, just to fill some arbitrary quota.

Now, some individuals may see this and think that I am advocating segregated schools. I am not. What I am advocating is that schools reflect the ethnic composition of the neighborhood in which they are located. If this leads to some inherently segregated schools, then the issue lies not with the school district to desegregate the school, but rather with the neighborhood itself. Not every neighborhood is a perfect mix of cultural and ethnic diversity. To expect that every neighborhood and its schools should be some perfect mix is ludicrous. Children expect to see their neighbors and the friends they play with after school in their neighborhood in their classes, and at their school. Neighborhood schools achieve this, and they do it without arbitrary, unnecessary quotas. Bring the schools back to the neighborhood and then work on ensuring quality teachers are in every school, that every building is modern and up to date, and that each school works with its local neighborhood to integrate the neighborhood with the school. That will produce greater change than any amount of forced student relocation, or forced school consolidation ever would.

What's Needed

We need schools that actually look and operate as schools, not prisons for children. Schools today are already different than when I completed elementary, junior high, and high school. We could walk freely in the school, did not have dress codes, and had no identification badges, no police in the school. We had fights, arguments, and personal lockers in the hallway. Teachers surveyed the halls between classes, ready to pounce on students who acted too far out of line. Instead, students now wear identification badges with their photograph on them, have armed, uniformed police roaming the hallways, pass through scanners and metal detectors as they enter the school, are prohibited from moving through the hallways unaccompanied, operate in locked buildings with few windows, and no guests, and are treated as inmates, rather than students. School is not prison, it should not feel like prison, and I, nor anyone else, should ever be able to make the comparison between the two.

Unfortunately, that is the current situation. The similarities are too many for schools to truly be places where students feel free to learn, instead, they are places where children are incarcerated for several hours per day and mandated that they learn certain information to "pass" a standardized exam. If we want better educated individuals, we need to treat children as children, not little inmates, and actually work to educate them, rather than force-feed information to them for an exam.

Colleges and Universities

College has become something of a rite of passage for many young Americans, whether it be through a traditional university or a community college, it is almost expected today that all adults attend college. I disagree with the belief that all adults should go to college, and feel that does a disservice to those who would be better suited to other vocations. For example, one does not require a college education to construct a home, till a field, repair a car, or do a host of other tasks which are very real and quite essential to the functioning of our society. In fact, do we really need a college degree to sell washing machines, run a store, manage a business, or serve in government? In many cases, I would argue that college education is not required for any of those tasks. In fact, for the vast majority of American history, all that was required to enter particular professions, such as law, was to study law under a lawyer (who followed the same training generally themselves previously) and pass the exam for admission to the Bar. Several of our presidents did just that. Some of our greatest scientific and creative minds had no formal college education, and yet we now place a college degree as the barrier for entry into even the most basic and banal of jobs. It is time to take a second look at why we send children to college in the first place, what they are there to do, and how that experience will benefit them going forward.

What I didn't learn in college

Generally speaking, at least in my own case, much of what I know I did not learn in college. I did not learn to write in college, nor how to read a map, how to spell, or how to reason or understand an argument (beyond the technical side of an argument, such as in a debate). I did not learn about politics, world events, or the way elections function in college. I did not learn any of the basic life skills in college, such as cooking, cleaning, basic sewing, home repair and maintenance, or about relationships. So what did I learn in college? I learned a great deal about very specific knowledge areas (mathematics, history, criminal justice, economics, as examples) but nothing that clearly taught me any particular 'job skills.' Yet, when I ask students why they are in college, the response I almost always get is "So that I can get a good job." That is entirely the wrong reason to be in college. College does not train you in job skills, but rather in knowledge areas. That does not mean that these knowledge areas do not provide a student with the ability to grasp job skills or to adapt to the needs of their employer, but it does not equate directly with "getting a good job."

In many cases, students I have spoken with have stated that they are fully aware that much of what they study in college has no bearing on their career after college, and that they fully expect to have to be retrained by their employer after college in how work is actually done, rather than what they learned in the classroom. If that is the case, then why go to college at all other than to get a piece of paper with some ink on it that you can put on a wall? This is not to say that all college educations are pointless – far from it, but what it does say is that there are certainly a significant number of students in college for entirely the wrong reasons, in programs that serve no purpose for them after they leave the university.

To be honest, a better scenario would be shifting the focus from the university to vocational schools for those who want to "find a good job" as training at vocational schools would be inherently focused on the needs of employers, graduating students would be prepared for the jobs that employers need to fill, rather than spending four years and thousands of dollars taking courses in content matter that they will forget as soon as the course is completed. Students need to be able to read, write, and do basic mathematics to succeed in life. They should also understand the history of the nation of which they are a citizen (in this case, the United States). They should also understand their rights and responsibilities as a citizen and their role in the political process. This is basic knowledge, most of which should have been met in the years of elementary and secondary education (and refined in the first year of training, even at a vocational school). Students learn their job skills and acquire the technical knowledge needed to succeed in the job of their choice thereafter.

So what about the university then? If a student wishes to do a particular job that does require advanced training in academic skills, such as a historian or an accountant, then the university is the right choice. That said, curriculum must change to accommodate the needs of two particular sets of students, those who are skills focused (depth focused) and those who are field focused (breadth focused).

Joshua R. Yates

The New College: Institutional and Curricular Reform

College, a term I have been using interchangeably with university, should be structured with two particular types of students in mind: Those who seek breadth and those who seek depth. It is possible to do both, but ultimately, that requires a much greater commitment in time, and once a student reaches graduate study they begin focusing on depth in one area, not breadth in many. To assume that all students truly required a breadth-focused experience is a disservice to those that want to focus entirely on one particular area. As the academy (another term for college or university) is populated by scores of faculty, most of which possess at least an M.A. or a Ph.D. (which essentially states that they are an expert on one niche area in one field), it is feasible that the institution could offer both breadth and depth focused educations at the undergraduate level as well as the graduate level. There is no reason not to.

If we want to change the idea of college from one that creates carbon copy graduates to one that focuses on training scholars, then we need to also change the institution itself. Colleges have become quite bloated in recent decades with administrators drawing more in salary at some colleges than the faculty. Furthermore, the explosion in the number of individuals in administrative staff positions has also increased spending, requiring ever increasing tuition hikes, paid for by students directly, their parents, or financed through huge amounts in student loans. The administrations of our colleges have grown quite massive from the extra money, and it is time for it to change.

First, it is paramount that universities perform internal audits, particularly performance audits, of their staff. I expect some resistance to this idea amongst these staff, but ultimately, if they were in the private sector and were performing below their expected level of productivity, they would be expected to increase performance or be terminated, or at best, reassigned. Too many times I have either witnessed, or been given reports from faculty and students at various schools incidents of staff chatting online, sifting through sites such as Facebook, or playing games, such as solitaire or mah-jongg tiles during work hours. If they are not being tasked at the appropriate level to justify their full-time status, then there is an obvious problem. Perhaps the workload does not justify that full-time slot, either way; a performance audit would identify those units within the university that were underperforming, and those who are overloaded. That is the first step in achieving a more efficient, more effective, university.

Step two is reallocation of resources more efficiently. This includes both changes to curriculum, but also changes to the structure of individual colleges within each university. Departments that logically should be combined should be if it is financially and logistically beneficial to do so. Let me provide an example. Suppose that you have two departments, history and political science, each separate. Suppose also that both departments have one staff member, who is currently being utilized at 50% for history and 35% for political science. These staff members are each earning $25,000 per year in salary. Let us assume also that the number of faculty in the department of history is double that of the department of political science. For ease of understanding, let us use 10 faculty for history and 5 for political science, with an average of $45,000 per year in salary. Let us also assume that both departments offer a number of courses that equals their faculty sizes (in terms of full-time equivalencies) – so 10 course in history, 5 in political science – all of which fill with 30 students per class. So, that means there are 300 students in the history courses, and 150 in political science courses total. Assuming each course is 3 credit hours and each student is paying $150 per credit hour (so $450 per student in these courses).

Therefore, the current expenses for faculty and staff in the history department are $475,000 per year on average. In political science, the total comes to $250,000 in staff and faculty salaries. Revenue from the history courses taught, assuming 300 students per semester for two semesters, totals $270,000. For political science courses taught in the same term, the total revenue is $135,000.

With each faculty member teaching only one course, the departments do not pay for themselves. Let's then assume each faculty member teaches two classes per semester, so 20 history courses, and 10 political science courses are taught per semester. Also assume they all fill, which doubles the revenues to $540,000 for history and $270,000 for political science. They both now are profitable, but just barely. It is also unlikely that history and political science together at a small-to-medium sized school, or even a large one, could fill 30 courses combined with 30 students in each course every semester. This is possible, but unlikely. In a more realistic scenario where only half fill or the number of students in the course is variable, is it unlikely either department would be able to remain profitable, allowing for raises for current faculty, hiring of new faculty, or expansion of the programs. This also assumes a fairly low salary for all faculty members, and also does not take into account that much of the tuition paid will be diverted to other units in the university for their costs as well. It is unsustainable for more profitable units of the university to continually subsidize unprofitable ones.

A consolidation of the two departments would shave $25,000 off the top, as one of the two staff members would have to be either reassigned or be released from employment by the university. Second, an examination of the faculty would need to be done. Faculty would need to be not only teaching more courses (regardless of tenure status, which we will discuss shortly) to more students, but actively recruiting new students to the program, ensuring that they graduate, and ensuring that research funds are coming into the department as well. Furthermore, faculty would need to be held accountable to ensuring that they are teaching often enough and are effective enough that they justify their remaining with the faculty. Some faculty may not like this approach, but ultimately, the university needs to be financially viable. Some units may operate at a loss in the short run, but they cannot operate at a loss in the long run and still justify themselves financially. Such a department would either need to be consolidated into a unit that is financially successful, be restructured in such a way as to be financially viable, or be eliminated. In general, restructuring or consolidation is - always - preferable to elimination of a department.

Cost savings in the above example could be found both from the elimination of the underperforming staff member, moving their work load to the remaining staff member (post-consolidation), cross-listing of courses between the now consolidated departments, and review of faculty based on performance, recruiting, research, and academic need. Faculty should be actively cultivating students who show an interest in their particular field into scholars under their guidance. Retirements are another way in which some departments can eliminate faculty to realize cost savings, but these retirements must not come at the cost of entire sub fields without a replacement already in place. Redundancies must be eliminated, faculty must be strategically positioned to provide the best education for students without being bloated in any particular area. Furthermore, faculty members must be champions of their sub fields, encouraging exploration of their sub fields and encouraging new scholarship by students, training and encouraging the next generation of scholars, who will ultimately be, their future replacements.

Universities must be prepared to make the hard decisions regarding their finances and ensuring that they are providing a solid value for the price. With the inevitable decrease in enrollments at traditional universities due to other elements of this plan (primarily, the refocusing on trade and vocational schools for those who are not seeking a purely academic education), it will be even more imperative that colleges and universities are prepared to examine their redundancies, eliminate inefficiency, and pursue a culture of knowledge, efficiency, and intellectualism that advocates for the pursuit of independent research and thought, rather than on "training for a job" or in mass producing graduates with little respect paid to the quality of or actual knowledge gained by those graduates.

When the costs of college, including the payments in interest on student loans, outweigh the benefits of the degree, coupled with the overwhelming number of graduates who state that they remember little to nothing from most of their general education courses (including courses from their major area of specialization), there is something wrong. We must have the will and resolve to make the needed changes if the university as an institution is to remain relevant and viable for the future. If the bureaucracy is too entrenched to pursue needed change, then perhaps it is time for new colleges and universities to form, having the motivation and drive to make these changes real. Perhaps it is time that we, as taxpayers and voters, exercise our will through the voting process to demand change at public universities through our elected lawmakers.

Moving beyond redundant staff, however, we must take note of the multiple layers of administration at nearly every university. Layering of administrators is normal in any bureaucracy. It provides a system, generally, of checks and balances and slows down processes to a degree. At times, this can be a good thing. For example, it can be a good thing to slow down demolition of a building in the event that you destroy the wrong building. In that case, you would have expected the bureaucracy to slow the process down and make sure they were removing the correct building before they brought in the wrecking ball. However, that same effect can also slow down needed reforms and can work to stall and eliminate the potential for reform in the institution. This aspect of bureaucracy has the potential to institutionalize both good and bad habits within the organization.

Bureaucracy is designed to protect itself from outside change. A good bureaucracy requires that "things" (such as procedures, policies, and funding among others) remain the same over time. It allows a certain degree of efficiency to develop for handling repetitive tasks. So, to introduce our changes, rather than dismiss or degrade bureaucracy as evil or ineffective, we need to remember that it can be effective – but we need to redesign the specifics of how the machine (the bureaucracy) operates. Similar to an engine, we can make modifications and upgrades to achieve better efficiency. While the end result remains the same with respect to the function of the engine, we can change the institution while maintaining the basic bureaucracy.

Getting back to the layers of administration at our universities, if we want to streamline our bureaucracy and reduce both inefficiency and expense, then we need to identify and consolidate redundant layers of administration. Do we really need, as an example, a chancellor, multiple vice chancellors, multiple directors (under the vice-chancellors) with their assistant directors, senior staff managers, and so forth to effectively operate the university? In some cases, these "supervisory"-titled individuals do not actually supervise at all, or if they do, they supervise one or two individuals. Honestly, this is a redundant expense, and in the same idea as eliminating staff that were redundant through reassignment or consolidation, so too should we do with administration and management. No level of administration, no job assignment, no task should be exempted from the eyes of performance auditors.

At the same time, we should reexamine the level of pay for administrators, as well as their benefits packages. In an era of total austerity, where we are asking taxpayers (and in this case, faculty, students, or their families) to shoulder a greater level of the burden in terms of costs and cuts, there is no reason why we should be offering "golden parachute" clauses for senior administrators upon their hiring. If we are struggling with our own budgets, there is no reason to support the institution of large-scale bonuses for senior administration as well. If we want transparency, which we should, then these expenses and the contract terms should be made clear and available to any who ask.

While the university should operate as a business enterprise, we must remember that this (except in the case of some private colleges) is a publicly funded business enterprise. Too often, many colleges and universities forget this, and act as though they were somehow entitled to their monies from the government, neglecting the fact that those funds were collected by tax revenues. Second, operating as a business, focused on ensuring at least break-even revenue, universities must lead by example with respect to efficiency and cost-control, but also on proactive use of resources (such as with maintenance and construction). They must remember that while a corporation might be able to pay a CEO several hundred percent more than their common employee, the universities, generally, are for-profit corporations. It cannot function the same. The pursuit of profit cannot be the motivation for the success of the university.

As I mentioned previously, I seek a breadth and depth system within the university, rather than the current general education and major/minor systems. I have yet to understand how paying to take a course in tennis or fencing truly helps one learn to be a successful accountant, historian, or geologist, for example. There is nothing wrong with providing students a foundation to build upon, but the university is not the place to go when you "don't know what you want to do with your life" or those who had to go to college because their parents told them to." The general education curriculum encourages this "go to college to explore" belief rather than a mentality of going to college because you want to become a chemist, or a geologist, or an accountant, or a museum curator, just to name a few examples. There is a place and a time for exploration, but it is not at the university. The university is a place to train scholars, scientists, and academics, not a place for students to learn tennis, bowling, and fencing and then have these listed as courses on their transcript. The fact you were good at playing tennis should not be a determinant in weighing your performance in college (GPA, grade point average) against your aptitude in chemistry, for example. Grade inflation and GPA boosting are problems enough without adding in these sorts of non-academic courses into the mix.

College is also not a place to take two years of entry-level courses in numerous fields before deciding you want to major in X, or taking a degree in "General Studies." I am sorry, but the idea of a college degree in "general studies" seems rather anathema to the point of the university in the first place. There should not be an academic degree that is given as some sort of consolation prize. This is not a game show where one receives a prize just for playing. The intent of the university, with regards to the granting of degrees, should be only to grant degrees which certify a particular level of academic knowledge and aptitude in a particular academic field, skills that position the graduate to take a position as a scientist, scholar, or proceed to graduate study for positions teaching and conducting research at a university or performing research or analysis for various institutions, academic, private, or otherwise. To grant degrees in "general studies" does a disservice to every student who holds a genuine degree in a major field from a given institution.

When I speak with students on campus at different schools, their desire is to focus on their area of specialty and do not understand why they would need to waste their money on courses wholly outside of their preferred specialization simply for some attempt at a "liberal arts" education which mandates that they do so. There is a difference from a well-rounded education and one which amounts to nothing more than "trash" course taken by students. A "trash" course is essentially a course that the student was mandated to take as part of a general curriculum, through which they regurgitate information on exams then forget the moment the course is concluded. To many students, this is simply a source of revenue for their university and does nothing to enhance the "quality" or "worth" of their program of study. Obviously some students do find some enjoyment out of particular courses outside their major field of specialty, but this should remain in the realm of personal hobbies and academic exploration by choice, not one of forced academic "study" and "worthless" tuition payments.

Worth is, of course, measured in the eye of the individual. What is worth more to me, in one way, may be worthless to another. Likewise with value. However, in this case, worth is measured in dollars spent and time spent, on return on investment. If I am studying to become an economist, all of the courses in classical British literature, unless I have some innate interest in the subject, are likely to fit the realm of worthless tuition. The same issue exists for a student of linguistics, for example, being induced to take courses in the natural sciences or engineering.

Returning to the ideas of breadth and depth courses, let me define and explain them further, so we can clear up any misconceptions that some might have about what I mean. When I refer to breadth, I am thinking of study in several areas of a particular discipline, or disciplines. So, as an example, let's suppose that a student wanted to study public relations as a field. Well, to fully understand public relations, you need to be able to write properly, so you'll need training in English skills, but you'll also need to understand journalism, marketing, communication (oral and written), mass and social media, and probably business management or political science, depending on how you wanted to focus yourself within the field. Beyond those, there are particular skills from within the discipline of public relations itself that you would need to know. So, from that glance, we can see the pure breadth of information, in general at least, that would need to be brought together to fully grasp such a field as public relations. In contrast, let us look at a student who wanted to study only American history. Well, to understand American history, one needs to understand basic military history, political science, economics, sociology, and be able to write properly, as a minimum. If the student wanted to focus in one particular element of American history, their coursework would focus to represent that. These students may benefit from courses in other areas, but those should be purely of their own choice.

So what, then, is a depth field? I will use a field such as geology as an example of a depth field. When I studied geology, many years ago, I required a working knowledge of mathematics, chemistry, some physics, and obviously, knowledge of geology. Other information was interesting, but ultimately, what I needed was being drawn from those fields. Focusing on petrology, which is the study of rocks, not oil, or the study of mineralogy, the study of minerals, not rocks, for example, would require different depth knowledge than someone studying hydrology, the study of water, or meteorology, the study of the atmosphere and weather. There would be no reason for any of these three fields to study at the same depth in one another, given their specializations. For example, a volcanologist, a geologist specialized in studying volcanoes, for example, would find their time better spent focusing on that particular specialty rather than studying Plato, formal logic or economics.

The difference between breadth studies and depth studies relies entirely on the level of specialization that the student desires from their program, rather than a hard and fast set of guidelines designed to churn out carbon-copy graduates in pre-formed molds. We must stop thinking of college as mass production of workers and look at college instead as a place where the next generation of scientists and scholars are trained. Not everyone is destined to be a scientist or scholar, and they should not be forced to be sent down that path. People should go to college to learn advanced skills in particular academic specializations, not to train for a "job."

If we intend for college to be an institution of higher learning, where our scientists and scholars of tomorrow are shaped and educated, then we need to set aside the idea of the perfectly well-rounded student, and remember why they are at the university in the first place. By the same token, if we reduce the vast number of general education courses, if not eliminating most of them outright as required, focusing instead on those essential to a student's field of study, then the value to the student is improved. With the outrageous costs of attendance today, this is more important than ever.

Online and On-Campus Education

As a student, being on-campus provides an atmosphere of learning that is generally unavailable in an online format. At the same time, the supposed flexibility of online education makes it a viable option for those who work or have other obligations. The problem is that there is a trend amongst those faculty who teach online that the online course should be identical to the seated course and be suited to fit their schedule and their desires, which is wholly contradictory to the premise of online education. If an individual enrolls in an online course, they expect to have the option to do the work at times which fit their schedule. Furthermore, they expect rapid responses to inquiries to the instructor and rapid responses to submitted work. Many times, online courses fail here on both counts. The course is either structured in such a way that it does not benefit the student in terms of time, where there may be required discussions during a particular time slot, which is not conducive to the student's schedule, or feedback from the instructor is so slow as to be considered virtually non-existent.

Several instructors, I am certain, will argue that this is never the case, and that they respond in due course to their students, within some arbitrary 24-hour or 48-hour window. That may be nice, but they are forgetting one key thing: it is not about them. The course must be focused on the student. Ultimately, without students enrolled, there is no course, and thus, no need for the faculty member in question to remain employed. Also, as this is an institution of education, the student is both attending to learn and is also the customer. Therefore, online courses, as with seated courses, are both educational environments, but also rooms of paying customers.

The trend of copying the seated class (on-campus, sitting in a classroom) format to the online realm has other negative consequences as well. For example, group work. As many students have told me, and I have experienced myself in the past, there is this persistent desire among some online faculty to require group work from their students. That may work in a traditional seated course; however, for online work, it is less useful. Often times, students who are forcefully assigned to work together will do so begrudgingly at best, with one student often shouldering more of the workload, while the other essentially becomes a free rider. These students who will likely never meet outside the online world, are concerned that their grade may suffer due to poor work on the part of the other individual(s). In any case, students in an online format should have the choice. If they wish to work together, then they should have the option to do so. Should they wish to work alone, that also should be viable. In an online course, there is a degree of independence desired by the student, and a desire for the course in question at a time, and in a manner, which best serves the student. This desire should not be circumvented simply because a given faculty member is either incapable or unwilling to alter the format and style of their course to fit an online format.

Many recent courses have made the shift to a reliance on forums and message boards as an alternative to (or "supplement to") classroom discussion. In many of the courses I have taken or seen, there is an insistence for group discussions among students. This is ironic as there are often little to no real discussions in seated courses, as forced discussion tends to produce lackluster commentary at best, or as an alternative, results in the same few individuals doing most of the talking.

Yet, in online courses, students are subjected to forced "discussions" on a regular basis, with required numbers of comments, posts, and word lengths, generally. Can one imagine if an instructor walked into a traditional classroom and demanded that every student respond to their question to the class and each comment needed to be at least two minutes in length, with a one-minute response to every other comment made by every other student in the class? The idea would rightly be absurd. Then why is it considered acceptable in an online format if it is obviously ridiculous in a seated format?

Then there are the lectures, or the (usual) lack of lectures. A common trend in online education is to have students read swaths of a given textbook or books and then to post their thoughts, comments, a review, some answers to particular questions, or perhaps respond to a quiz or assignment list, with little to no actual lecture given. In a seated class, it would still be expected that students would have read the required material, this is obvious, however, they would not be expected to be instant experts and be able to competently discuss the material without context, perspective, and insight on what they read from their instructor. That is why the instructor is there, and is being paid. If students were able to glean all they needed from reading the books and determining for themselves what it means, then all they would need is to pay for a reading list and some books. There would be no need for the instructor at all. If online education is intended to be just that – education – then the educating needs to be occurring, and that generally means some level of lecture (even typed) to help students to understand the material, put it into context (both generally and with respect to the topic of the course itself), and to help students relate this material to other material they have read.

When you have students respond to questions on exams, essays, or other papers, the level of knowledge and understanding should be expected to be thorough, and the questions should be asked appropriately to allow students to extrapolate on what they have learned and address new situations and new ideas as extensions of the material studied. Student "discussions" are no substitute for the guidance, insight and knowledge, presented by an instructor. By virtue of being the instructor, the faculty member is expected to have mastery over the information, and thus, should take the leadership role After all, that is why students are paying for their services and not simply buying a reading list and some books to learn the material on their own.

There is a term, commonly used when discussing online education called "social-constructivism." What this means, generally speaking, is the belief that one learns more through interactions as a group, both learning from the group as a whole as well as from any content that individuals are reading separately. Therefore, the goal is to push group interaction and group activity, rather than individualized activity or individualized work. I have seen this concept being utilized in many online courses I have taken myself, but also in most of the "best practices" literature regarding creation of online courses. If you would not demand this level of interaction in a seated course, where success should really be based on an individual's own work, not on some collective group effort, then why demand it of people who will never see one another, and who are working separately online.

I do not argue that group discussion can, at times, provide creative new insight on particular topics. What I do argue with is that it is not the ONLY means by which individuals can achieve understanding and competence on a topic. As an individual, I want to be free to do my own work, be graded for my own effort and my own understanding, and be able to do this without having to worry about if another individual that I am paired with understands the content at the same level that I do. Furthermore, why should my work, which might be of higher quality, support another student whose work is lower quality? In economics, we call this the issue of the free rider. In any group environment, there will inevitably be the presence of a free rider, an individual who wants to skate by on the success of the group while their own lack of contributions goes largely unnoticed. Therefore, my complaint with the current "best practices" is also one which questions the validity of social-constructivism as the primary focus for online teaching.

So what would a quality online course look like? What is the real solution? First, you need enough textbooks or supplemental information to provide the foundation for any topics being discussed. This is no different than a seated course. However, additional supplemental information could always be supplied by email or through some sort of education software (such as Blackboard or WebCT, two commonly used educational software platforms). Second, individual faculty need to prepare quality lectures for each week of work. These lectures should assume that students have read the materials, and therefore should not rehash what was contained within the readings, but supplement them in a way which provides more clarity or understanding of the material. If they want to go one step further, recorded lectures (audio or video) would be a great supplement to a written lecture. Have these lectures available to listen at the convenience of the student at a time that best fits their schedule.

Faculty should also communicate with students through a forum on any questions that they might have. The forum then substitutes for the in-class questions that students ask of the professor. At that point, each week should require a short paper, answering questions by the professor based on the readings and the lecture(s). That will allow for the student to synthesize what they have read and to apply that information to particular questions. These questions should range from basic knowledge questions up through the higher levels of Bloom's taxonomy, to encourage students to look deeper at the content they have read, as well as integrating previously learned content.

Student interaction is less critical in an online course given the impersonal nature of the classes themselves; however, it should be an option for those who wish to do so. As an instructor, posting a question on the forum for all to answer and discuss is a good idea, but it should not be seen as a gauge to measure student knowledge or involvement. Some students never speak up in seated classes, and that is perfectly alright. Not everyone will participate in discussion, and they should not be forced to do so if they are uncomfortable with it, especially in an online class. What is important is the ability of the student to understand the information, to be able to synthesize it, and then to apply it to new situations that differ from the examples they have been given before. These small changes would produce more interesting and exciting online courses.

With a real solution for online education, now let's examine on-campus education. In general, courses on-campus tend to be held during the work day, but can also be held at night. This said, the course offerings at night always tend to be more restrictive than those held during the day. If there are full programs both during the day and at night, there is a tendency to keep the two wholly separate and to prevent students from one side from taking courses on the other. This was the case with my undergraduate degree. This wall of separation also tends to create a two-caste society within the campus, as you have the students who attend traditionally, during the day, and then those "others" who come on-campus at night for class.

Add to this mix the graduate-level course listings. These, again, differ based on the school as to when they are offered. For some schools, daytime courses are offered, others, and the more common of the two, are offerings of graduate courses at night. Offering graduate courses at night fits well for two groups in particular. First, graduate students who are working as teaching assistants, and thus, may teach their own courses during the day. Second, for those individuals who work during the day and want to continue their education.

There is a third group that appears left out in this – graduate students who want to attend full-time, but are not teaching or graduate assistants – and have no other outside employment. These students often want to work as a graduate assistant on-campus but were not selected for a position. Is the solution then to provide all graduate students with assistantships? Perhaps, but there is a caveat there, that if all graduate students are hired as assistants, then they need to be teaching courses, or assisting with research. As we hire more graduate students as assistants, and therefore, as instructors, then we reduce the need for adjuncts, and thus can realistically pay assistants more than the sub-poverty level wages paid by many universities.

Inevitably, if we are discussing increased numbers of, and pay for, graduate assistants, then we must address what I call "megaclasses." These are the giant lecture classes that some of us remember, with hundreds of students in a cavernous lecture hall. The instructor will be at the bottom of the pit with either a chalkboard (or whiteboard for dry-erase markers instead of chalk) or a overhead projector. They give a lecture as though they are speaking to no one and the entire event amounts to, essentially, a textbook wired for sound. The classes, while great revenue generators for colleges do a huge disservice to the students actually sitting in the class. Rather than sitting in the lecture, why not simply record the entire lecture, tape it to the front of the textbook, have the student listen to the lecture and then show up to take an exam. The end result is identical. If we want real instruction and real learning, then we must acknowledge that the "textbook wired for sound" model does not work. It does not work in lectures of 400 students, nor does it work in lectures of 40 students.

I am reminded of a course that I took in graduate

macroeconomics. In this case, we were being asked to examine the impact of one particular variable, ATM machines in this case, on other variables. Bear in mind, none of the models we were studying had a variable for ATMs built in, so we had to learn to adapt what we had learned to solve the question. This is just one example, but if the ability to expand beyond a given example and to understand the information on a more intuitive level is the goal, then colleges must teach appropriately. We cannot expect any student to simply gain some understanding of a topic on a deeper level simply because of a once-over, "textbook wired for sound" lecture, or that the student will immediately understand how to put the knowledge into context and appropriately apply it to other situations without guidance. That is what faculty are there to do: to teach, to guide, and to help facilitate understanding and the ability to apply knowledge learned to broader situations. It is the entire point of Bloom's taxonomy; something everyone in education should be familiar with.

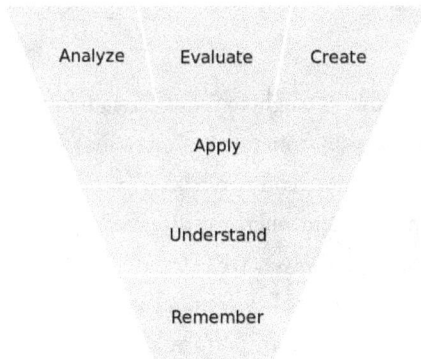

Bloom's Taxonomy

So, what is the solution then to "megaclasses?" The honest answer is smaller classes. Somewhere up to 40 students is still acceptable for a large class, and will happen in some instances. However, classes of 80 or 100 or 400 students are entirely inappropriate. It does not matter if the class is broken up into smaller subsections of 20 or 30 students if the main lecture has 400 students. At that point it's better to break the class into multiple separate sections, each taught by graduate students. In doing so, you are encouraging a better use of your graduate students, keeping them engaged and helping to get them classroom experience. This is workable, and despite administration claiming that the overhead from the faculty required to teach these classes would be prohibitive, it is not. Graduate students can easily fill the gap, as could currently underutilized faculty members. The true reason for resistance is the loss in profit margins from these "megaclasses." Furthermore, this benefits students by eliminating redundant "discussion" sections (taught by graduate students) in addition to attending the "lecture" section (usually taught by a professor, in the "textbook wired for sound" style).

Tenure

Tenure was always taught to me as a means by which academics were granted protection from retribution so that they might conduct research which was more controversial. This seems perfectly logical to have in an environment where the threat of retribution might stifle legitimate research. However, what tenure has become is a catch-all term to allow faculty not to conduct controversial research, but instead, to be protected from performance, research and teaching requirements. To be protected from accusations of prejudice, racism, sexism, favoritism, or other issues. To be protected from bringing in the revenue through teaching courses (due to reduced teaching loads with the courses farmed out to adjuncts, instructors, or graduate assistants) or conducting relevant research to complete books and academic papers in a timely fashion. Now, this might seem a bit too generalized, and it likely is, but it is intended to illustrate the common issues with the tenure system and its inflexibility or lack of accountability.

In discussions, for example, with a faculty member at a private university, it was mentioned that their tenure system required faculty to be reviewed every few years, with the result of each review being as follows: first review is to grant tenure (5 years into employment). The second review (at 10 years of employment) is to ensure the faculty member is doing research, teaching properly, etc., with issuance of a warning if they are not performing adequately. The third review (at 15 years into employment) is the same as the second, with this stage warranting a reprimand if the faculty member was already issued a warning. This begs the question: where is the risk for the faculty member? So they fail to perform at the level required, but they are not at risk to losing tenure until 20 years into employment? At that point, they may well be close to their retirement or have moved to another university. If they were employed at a private company, they would likely have seen swifter action for poor performance than waiting 20 years to do so. The lost revenues alone make the system discussed above worthless for ensuring faculty performance, turning tenure into a shield for poor performance.

Furthermore, the wall of tenure has driven administrators to look for alternatives to actually hiring tenure-track faculty. Rather than pay market wages for tenure-eligible faculty, vast numbers of universities turn to graduate students, adjuncts, or instructors, all of whom are paid, generally, below market wage and typically offered few or no benefits. A graduate student, paid appropriate living wages along with tuition and fee waivers, can be a valuable asset to a department by teaching lower-level courses. After all, many graduate students are planning to teach at the college level, and therefore it is good training for those students to learn how to teach properly by doing it in a setting where they can learn proper educational methods and techniques and be mentored by faculty they are already working with in their studies before they obtain their first post-graduate teaching assignments. This improves the quality of teaching in their respective field and helps to ensure that when they arrive at their first posting, they are better prepared to step into the classroom with fewer of the stops and starts common to new faculty members teaching for the first or second time.

Adjuncts, by contrast, are typically individuals who work in careers other than in the academy, perhaps as an accountant, attorney, or police officer, or some other form of traditional employment. They often are local experts with years of practical experience in the field. Adjuncts can bring valuable knowledge and experience, but they typically have less time available to meet with students outside of the classroom, and so are less available than a tenure-track faculty member, an instructor, or even a graduate student. Like graduate students, adjuncts tend to earn very low pay for their teaching, usually a minimal, flat amount per class, or in some cases, an amount per student. This arrangement always benefits the university more than the adjunct, and due to the time constraints, tends to provide less benefit to students as well.

Instructors are faculty who are generally not eligible for any kind of tenure system. They are treated, normally, as being "permanent adjuncts" in a sense. Pay is almost universally below market wages and the individuals are typically reminded that they are not tenure eligible and are classified as "temporary." These individuals may also be called "lecturers" at some institutions, but this is not always the case, as some lecturers are tenured. What makes instructors different is that they often times are either ABD (ABD stands for "all but dissertation," which means they have completed their Ph.D.

classes and exams, but have yet to finish their dissertation) or hold a Master's degree only.

This is not always the case, but it is fairly common. Often times they are tasked to teach a full course load each term, focusing mostly on teaching, rather than research. The only difference between an "instructor" and an "assistant professor" is usually a significant pay gap and the possible lack of a Ph.D. by the instructor. Student experience is largely the same, instructional effectiveness is largely the same, and focus on professional development is largely the same. Universities tend to receive a greater profit from using instructors rather than tenure-track faculty, since the instructor is paid less, has (often) no benefits, and are usually contract employees.

If tenure were reformed from the current "job protection" system that is has become, to protection from retaliation for controversial research, there would be no reason to maintain the arbitrary differences between instructors and assistant professors. The field could be equalized to allow for the hiring of instructors as permanent faculty with the option to advance into "clinical assistant professor" roles (clinical faculty are typically individuals who may or may not possess a Ph.D. but have experience in the field and in the classroom) which opens up the doors to teaching to those individuals who possess experience outside of the university, rather than strictly new Ph.D. graduates. These clinical faculty would bring greater real world experience to the university, enriching students' experiences.

In the end, this is a viable solution to change the current tenure system. In this case, faculty would be reviewed to determine if they were meeting their performance or research goals annually, allowing universities to promote or demote faculty accordingly in rank, and also encouraging quality research and quality instruction. Tenure should not be about job protection from poor performance. Every faculty member should be examined to determine if they are both efficient and effective. These changes should help foster this shift in the industry.

In addition to tenure at the college-level, there are also issues of the use of the term "tenure" for elementary and secondary schools as well. Certainly tenure of service can mean seniority, but that definition is not what was intended at the collegiate level, and should not apply at the elementary or secondary levels either. Given that the intention of tenure should be to protect the faculty member from retribution as a result of their research work, it is difficult to see how the idea of "tenure" fits instances outside of the university. For elementary and secondary school teachers, the proper term should be seniority, rather than tenure.

Seniority and Educational Staff Policies

When I worked in management in a company in which our laborers were unionized, it was imperative for all of us in management to remember the seniority of each employee under our supervision. Failure on our part to respect seniority could mean a grievance filed against the offender by the employee, which I generally tried to avoid. However, when it came to productivity, while some of my most senior employees were not only efficient and some of my best producers, there were also those with less seniority who were equally as effective, if not more so. Seniority was a poor measure of performance. In fact, if I was forced to send home all of my lowest seniority employees my productivity would likely plummet. The key here was to combine respect for seniority with a drive for performance.

I mention this story as an example of how many school districts are failing to do the same They look only at seniority, granting tenure (though in my mind an inappropriate use of the term 'tenure') and then failing to recognize the importance of also focusing on performance. When all of your staffing decisions are entirely based on seniority, you are placing an arbitrary cap on your own success. You might terminate employment of your highest producers, or your best employees, and retain employees who acted as free riders on your high producers, essentially dead weight, simply because of seniority. Don't take this to mean that all individuals with high seniority fall into this category of free riders. There are individuals who attempt to go unnoticed as free riders at all levels of seniority. My entire point is to illustrate the failure of a "seniority-only" system as a means of determining staffing decisions.

Alternatively, it should be expected of all elementary and secondary educators, just as with the tenure reforms at the university-level, that they sit before a panel of their peers, and demonstrate they have continued their education on educational techniques, subject knowledge, and that they have mastery of the appropriate metrics to support their effectiveness in the classroom. Does this mean teach to a test? No. If you are teaching to a test, or some exam, then you are doing a disservice to yourself, your students and the profession. Rather than teaching to a test, we should truly be measuring that students have mastered content and can demonstrate their mastery. This means that educators must work to guide students to thinking at a more complex level on the subject matter, that the questions students can answer are higher-order questions on Bloom's Taxonomy. Properly educated, our students can handle the challenge. It is time we gave them the opportunity to be challenged, and to succeed.

Joshua R. Yates

Taxes

Taxes. Always a topic that many people wish to ignore, others decry as abhorrent to the idea of freedom and liberty, and others still claim taxation as a privilege for wealth and individual prosperity. What is always missing is that in the United States, income tax was not a reality until the twentieth century. Indeed, prior to that time, the very idea of a tax on income seemed inconsistent with wanting to encourage people to work. Once an income tax was implemented, it was designed as a tax only on the wealthy. Later it was expanded to include individuals at all income levels.

A viable, and oft forgotten alternative to income taxes are consumption taxes, and also VATs (or Value Added Tax). Consumption taxes, also called sales taxes, are applied at the time an individual consumes a good, such as when they are purchasing a product or service. Income is not taxed when it is earned, only when it is spent. This allows consumption taxes to incorporate future and current wealth as taxable in ways that income taxes cannot do. Value Added Taxes (or VATs), a European alternative to consumption taxes, are applied at each stage in a products development, and are typically compounded over time, as the new price for each stage in development includes all previous VATs. For example, what this means is that when I mine the ore, which I then sell to a smelter, a VAT is applied and is included in the price of the ore. Then, after the ore is smelted and sold to another firm, the VAT is calculated again, and includes

45

the VAT from the previous stage as well in it. So, if the mined ore cost $1,000, and had a 10% VAT applied, the price would have been $1100. Now, the smelted ore is being sold for an additional $1000, so $2,100, with a 10% VAT, of $2,310. Notice that each stage is factoring in all previous VATs from prior stages. Suppose that a third manufacturer uses the new smelted ore to create a car chassis – the new chassis has a VAT applied again when it is sold to the automobile manufacturer. Finally, another VAT is applied when the automobile manufacturer produces the new car that the consumer buys from a dealer. In each case, the tax is being passed on to the next consumer.

The primary difference between VATs and consumption taxes are in how they are applied. While the VAT is applied at each stage in the production, the consumption tax is only applied once, when the finished product is sold to the consumer. There are some countries that employ both consumption taxes and VATs, which is not something that I support here in the United States. If we can achieve desired revenue without additional taxes, then we should seek to do so. Our current tax system is ridiculously complicated and needlessly so. It is used as a political tool to benefit allies and harm political enemies. This chapter will discuss two alternatives to the current tax system, one is a modified income tax, and the other is a consumption tax plan, called the FairTax.

Income Taxes

An income tax can be progressive, which is to say that it does not more-heavily impact those on the lower end of the wage scale more adversely than those on the upper end. This is a highly simplified definition of a progressive tax, but it is accurate. Regressive taxes, by comparison, harm those on the lower end of the scale proportionally more than those on the upper end. An example of this would be if someone who earned $35,000 in one year were made to pay taxes at 35% while one who earned $50 million paid taxes at 10%. While the amount paid by the one whom earned $50 million is obviously higher in terms of actual total dollar amount paid, the impact on the one who earned less is proportionally higher by percentage of total income, making the tax regressive.

Now that we have a basic definition to work from for progressive taxes and regressive taxes, let's take a look at our current tax system. In terms of the percentages, the current tax system appears progressive. Individuals with higher incomes, at least on the surface, do have a higher tax percentage than those with lower incomes. That is, until one looks beyond the basic rates and factors in deductions, capital gains taxes, as well as the FICA (and SECA for those who are self-employed) tax, which funds Social Security and Medicare. Interestingly, the social security portion of FICA/SECA taxes caps out at $108,000 in income, meaning someone who earned $108,000 and another who earned $1 billion in income both paid the same amount in social security taxes. Therefore, using our definitions from above, it is clear that FICA/SECA is wholly regressive. Furthermore, it is likely that the individual who has significantly higher income may also have a greater number of tax deductions to employ, thus reducing their tax burden, effectively turning what would be a progressive tax system into one that is, in terms of proportionality, regressive on all levels.

The question becomes then, why do we accept such a system that rewards those who have the highest incomes with the greatest opportunities for tax relief while punishing those who are in the center (or bottom) of the income ladder with a proportionally (by percentage of total income) greater tax burden? There is no simple answer to this question. For some, the issue is one of powerlessness. The tax code is enormous, and in many cases, unwieldy for anyone who is not a trained accountant or lawyer to grapple with. In my view, however, this is the equivalent to stacking the deck. It only benefits those with the knowledge and the financial means to exploit its intricacies and loopholes. This is simply unacceptable in my mind, and it is time that Americans have a tax system that works for everyone, rather than for some of us. It is time to make real changes to the tax system in the United States.

The only way to enact the kind of change that our tax code needs is to repeal the current tax code entirely and implement a new system. Likewise, this type of change would need to be done, not gradually, but all at once. Any graduated implementation only exacerbates the punishing nature of the current system. I do not agree with the idea that we need to make such a change over a long period of time, as this myth only drags out the problem longer than is necessary. The belief that bureaucracies cannot be made to change quickly is not one that I adhere to, and I believe that such a policy (one that holds that a bureaucracy moves at unrealistically slow speeds) only increases the chances for that bureaucracy to do what it does best: looking busy and doing nothing. The stakes are too high, and this is our money. Bureaucracy exists to serve, whether it be government or corporate, and it must be made to do so efficiently and effectively. There is no alternative.

The first option for a new tax system that I propose is a five-tiered tax system, with each tier paying one flat percentage. I will elaborate on those percentages in a moment, but let us take a look at how this five-tiered tax system is different from the current system. First, the five brackets allow for lower taxes to be paid by the lowest incomes, and the highest bracket to pay its proportionally higher fair share, based on ability to pay, in terms of raw percentage. Thus, it is, by our earlier definition, progressive. Remembering that the current tax system, which has higher base percentages for higher incomes still lends itself to becoming regressive by offering vast tax deductions which benefit those on the upper end more than those on the lower end. To that question, I suggest the elimination of all deductions and a drastic limitation on tax credits. With this elimination, let us all keep in mind that in an individual income tax, all individuals should pay as individuals. There would be no benefit to filing as a couple nor as a "head of household." An individual's tax burden is their own, and it is each individual's responsibility as citizens to pay their part, without a penalty for choosing to remain single or a bonus for being married, or because a taxpayer has children. Individuals who are married, in a partnership (including civil union) may choose to file their returns together, but they each pay their own separate tax portion.

If one taxpayer, filing together with another individual, has overpaid while the other has underpaid, then that overpaying taxpayer could apply their refund against the other's remaining tax burden. It would be a choice on the part of the two individuals that makes good logical sense, and provides a more practical benefit to joint filing, rather than a financial benefit to doing so. In this way, married, single, partnership or civil union, children or not, it does not matter. This tax system is more fair, and progressive, for all taxpayers.

The New Income Tax Brackets

Let's get straight to the numbers then. This new plan functions with five separate and distinct income categories (by percentage): 10, 15, 20, 25, and 30%. To ensure that this plan encourages growth of incomes at all levels, while ensuring that those who are at the lowest end of the income ladder are not taxed back into poverty, an income floor must be established. This floor should be 300% of the federal poverty income level, plus the minimum tax rate (10%) combined, or (as of 2011, for one person) $35,937. Since everyone files as an individual in this system (even if they file a joint return), each individuals income is subjected individually to the floor for a determination of tax liability. So, if I earn $32,000 this year and my spouse earns $65,000, the only taxes we would be liable for would be the taxes due against her income as mine are exempt (see table). Credits can be claimed against her tax liability, however, since we are jointly filing, even though no credits can be applied against my zero liability.

There would be no additional incentives, with respect to dependents, as it is likely that individuals with dependents may qualify for at least one of the tax credits, and thus would have some additional tax relief through credits, rather than by increasing the income floor. What I mean by floor is that if an individual, after tax, would have been reduced in income to below $35,937 (based on the calculations above) then they would pay no tax, and would also not be eligible for any tax credits. As their income is already exempt from taxation, credits would be effectively moot as the tax burden cannot be lower than zero. However, once their income exceeds the floor they would then be both subject to tax, but also eligible for tax credits.

Once income exceeds the floor, an individual would pay 10% tax on their income until they reached the next threshold, $50,000. After $50,001, the tax rate on total income changes to 15% until the next threshold is reached, $100,000. This continues for each tax bracket (shown in table), with the taxes being assessed via a simple calculation of gross income multiplied by the tax percentage. Unlike the current tax system which taxes different sections and types of income at different rates, this system assesses the individual only at whatever their total income was and assesses the relevant tax rate, not each lower bracket for that portion of income. What this means is that instead of assessing the income from 35,937 to 50,000 at 10% and then the portion from 50,001 to 100,000 at 15%

and so forth, if the individual earned $267,000 that year, the tax on their whole income, is 25%, or $66,750 before any tax credits are applied. The simplified calculations mean that filing returns will be less time consuming, less confusing, and less prone to error than they are today. Instead of several hundred pages of documents to sort through, the tax return could be reduced to only a few pages. The instructions could also be condensed and made clearer through the elimination of convoluted tax calculation schedules and deductions.

Income Range (in dollars)	Tax Rate
0 – 35,937	EXEMPT
35,937 – 50,000	10%
50,001 – 100,000	15%
100,001 – 250,000	20%
250,001 – 500,000	25%
500,000+	30%

Table 1: Tax brackets under the proposed income tax system

This system also eliminates the alternative minimum tax (or AMT), as there is no reason for specific penalties for individuals who earn greater incomes. AMT is, according to the Internal Revenue Service, a "separately figured tax that eliminates many deductions and credits." Essentially, the AMT increases tax liability for an individual who might other pay lower taxes. With the elimination of tax deductions, loopholes, and other miscellaneous means by which income can be shielded from taxation, those individuals who earn significant incomes will already pay their fair share of the tax burden. Penalty taxes, such as the alternative minimum tax, become irrelevant and thus, should be eliminated. We must also remember that many individuals who possess great wealth do not earn income in a traditional manner – they earn it through dividends or as corporate stock, which has its own tax rate (capital gains) outside of the regular income tax rate. If we want to encourage greater investment both by those with great wealth and by people working to create wealth, then it is incumbent upon us to reform the capital gains tax and eliminate the AMT.

Income Tax Credits - Few and Limited

So, no deductions at all? That's right — no deductions. Deductions are treated, under the current tax system, as reductions in income for the purpose of determining what tax rate an individual pays. Deductions must be eliminated if we are to tax individuals at their true rate of income and account for their real tax burden, rather than some legislatively constructed definition of income as part of a convoluted tax code. Instead of deductions, this income tax system uses a specific set of tax credits, with changes to the credits under this code requiring a super-majority in each chamber to be made. Tax credits are items that reduce your actual taxes owed. The goal here is to prevent Congress from using the tax code as a way to benefit friends and hinder enemies. The tax code has grown to its enormous size as a result of these niche perks and penalties that are passed by our Congress each year. We must halt this inappropriate use of the tax code as a tool of patronage and bring fairness to the system for all taxpayers. These few, particular credits can help along the road to the achievement of that goal.

Tax Credits

Encouraging savings for the future is always good policy. As such, a tax credit for individuals saving money in long-term investments, such as IRA accounts, should be available, in a 1:1 ratio, up to $5,000 per year. The goal with this credit is to encourage individuals to place portions of their wages into these retirement savings accounts. By encouraging individual saving toward retirement, it pushes Americans into a better financial position by the time that they reach retirement. Obviously this will be more effective for younger workers than for those who are closer to retirement, but any improvement in saving for retirement (as a society) is a good improvement.

Another credit would be for school tuition. In this case, either tuition for one's own education or for children who are still dependents. This would provide a means by which individuals who are currently in college, considering it, or are considering a job retraining program or (some additional education to improve their current job) the means by which to reduce that expense from their tax. Parents who send their children to private schools would also qualify for the tax credit. This is a win-win situation for everyone involved. When people are able to improve their employment situation (either by finding employment, retraining for new employment, or by promotion within their current employment), their income is likely to improve or become more stable, ensuring better, long-term revenue through tax. These two credits alone are investments in our nation's future, which ultimately is what taxes are intended to do.

One particular deduction I would eliminate, that must be mentioned, is the home mortgage interest deduction. I understand the argument that has been made by some economists that this deduction does not actively encourage home ownership among those at the lower-to-middle range of the income ladder. Intuitively, this logic makes sense. If you can afford to purchase a home, with a larger loan amount, you are already in a higher tax bracket, and thus will net a larger deduction. The deduction is itself rather regressive, and intuitively seems counterproductive to the goal of encouraging home ownership. Therefore, we need to think in terms of alternatives that would produce this desired effect.

Rather than deducting the interest paid, which amounts to, in effect, reduction of tax burden on an individual because they are paying interest to a bank (effectively a tax subsidy to banks), the benefit (the credit) should be in owning a home itself, mortgaged or not. Other nations, such as Canada and the United Kingdom, do not allow mortgage interest to be deducted, and their citizens do not appear to be suffering for it. If we want to encourage home ownership in the United States, then our leaders need to offer a direct, standardized tax credit for owning a first, or primary, home. To be equitable, this credit should be based around a national median of home values (not local or regional), taken over a five year period (individual year medians) and then averaged for five years. The credit could increase if the national median home value five-year average increased, but could also decrease as well. To ensure that this national median house value would not plummet in any one given cycle, a provision would need to be applied to cap the decline to no greater than 10% of the last given averaged median valuation for purposes of taxation.

The ultimate goal with this credit is to foster the growth of home ownership among the middle and lower ends of the income ladder, and thus the credit must reflect that. Knowing that the credit is based on the median home value nationally, we then declare the credit, annually, as a percentage of that value. A credit of 2.5% of the five-year average of median home value would be fair. As an example, let's suppose that the averaged median home value was $150,000. Then, 2.5% of that is $3,750. Thus, in this case, owning a home nets the individual taxpayer a tax credit of $3,750 against their tax burden annually. Regardless of how far along they are in their mortgage or if they even have a mortgage at all, what their income is, or the value of their individual home, the tax credit is the same. All that matters is that they own a primary home. This type of credit alone would provide an incentive to own a home, rather than to rent, and would change the thinking from one of indebtedness being a benefit to one of ownership and property as being the benefit, regardless of indebtedness. In fact, continuing to own property after paying off any debts would be incentivized as it would continue to provide the benefit. Additionally, couples who own their home together can each claim the credit, applying the credit individually against their individual tax burden.

Further credits against tax would be provided through two particular bonds. The first credit would be for the amount of what I refer to as infrastructure bonds purchased that year. Thus, the government provides individuals with a mechanism for redirecting a portion of what they would have paid in tax entirely toward infrastructure development. A worthwhile investment in our nation, and thus the amount spent buying infrastructure bonds, is credited against the tax burden. Second, a credit would be provided for purchasing debt bonds. These new bonds would be available for purchase to allow Americans to effectively buy existing government debt. Thus, individuals who wished to purchase these bonds would be able to also apply the amount against their tax burden as a credit.

This system strictly taxes, by percentage based on your total income, for every individual, and then only reduces that tax burden through credits. The goal here is to treat income as what an individual actually earns and not one that is affected by a plethora of deductions, reductions, havens, or legal and accounting legerdemain. It evens the playing field for all individuals and makes sure that individuals are paying their fair share, regardless of where they fall in the spectrum. Furthermore, it ensures that the tax code does not unfairly penalize individuals, while encouraging habits such as saving, investing in our nation, and the acquisition of real property as a means of generational wealth growth, thus raising the long-term wealth level for all Americans. It makes the tax code easier to understand, and easier to enforce, reduces incentives to evade one's tax burden, and eliminates the need or purpose of intrusive tax audits.

I am sure that some of you are probably saying, "This sounds nice and all, but what about other taxes beyond Federal Income Tax? What about FICA, estate, or capital gains taxes? What about corporate taxes?" These questions are all legitimate and will be answered in order, including corporate taxes, which I will focus on in their own section.

FICA and SECA - Entitlements Taxes

First up we have the FICA tax, formally called the Federal Insurance Contributions Act tax (or in its more demystified definition, the payroll taxes which fund Social Security and Medicare). For those readers who are self-employed, this tax is called the SECA tax, or Self-Employment Contributions Act tax. Both carry the same percentages of tax contributions (overall), aside from temporary reductions, of 15.3% (broken down as 12.4% for Social Security and 2.9% for Medicare). In the case of FICA, this 15.3% is split between the employer and the employee, with each paying half. For SECA, the entirety is paid by the self-employed individual taxpayer. It is an illusory difference that one pays more than the other, given that the one who is self-employed is acting as both employer and employee, and thus must cover the "invisible" half that the regular employer is paying for their employee.

Another aspect of FICA and SECA is that there is a cap on income that is taxed within the system. Currently, income beyond what is called the Wage Base ($106,800) is not taxed under these taxes. So, someone who earns $10 million dollars in income this year pays the same dollar amount as someone who earned

$106,800 for the Social Security percentage of FICA. The slice for Medicare, 2.9%, however, is not capped on income, and so it is a flat tax against all income, at all levels. Only the Social Security portion has the cap. For taxpayers, both the FICA and SECA taxes are a penalty for working; these taxes are harsh, and extremely regressive. As with the Federal Income Tax, and the overhaul of the entitlements programs I suggest in a subsequent chapter, it is also time to consider transforming how we fund Social Security and Medicare.

<u>*Wage Base*</u>
(maximum taxed income)
Before = $106,800
After = Unlimited *(income from all sources)*

	Medicare		Social Security			
Income	*Before*	*After*	*Before*	*After*	*TOTAL (Before)*	*TOTAL (After)*
Below $50,000	2.9%	3.0%	12.4%	7%	15.4%	10%
$50,001 - $100,000	2.9%	3.0%	12.4%	8%	15.4%	11%
$101,000 - $250,000	2.9%	3.0%	0%	9%	2.9%	12%
$250,001+	2.9%	3.0%	0%	10%	2.9%	13%

Creating a system that is progressive for taxation, but still provides adequate funding for these entitlement programs is challenging, but not impossible. I have heard proposals to simply remove the income cap on the 12.4% tax for Social Security. However, this does nothing to make the tax more progressive or to make it fairer for individuals at all income levels. It would be a flat tax, but still proportionally hurt those on the lower end of the income ladder unjustly. A better version would be to change the structure of the system entirely, including the percentage rates. So, just as with the Federal Income Tax system discussed previously, I also suggest a graduated percentage rate system for FICA and SECA taxes as well. It is slightly more complicated than only a flat percentage rate with a cap or even a flat percentage rate with no upper cap, but does make the system more progressive with incomes.

This alternative tax structure for the Medicare portion of the FICA/SECA would be a flat 3% tax for all income levels. It would not increase or decrease and would remain the same as it is at the present in style. Rather than a 2.9% base rate and any additional surcharge rates, it changes to 3% for all – easy, fair, and consistent with the present. The Social Security portion would change entirely. For those in the 10% tax bracket (discussed previously), or those earning $50,000 or below, their rate, split between themselves and their employer as it is now, would become 7%. For those in the next bracket, 15%, or $50,001-$100,000 of income, their rate would be 8%. The 20% tax bracket would pay 9% and the highest two brackets pay 10%.

Reduced payments by those on the lowest end of the spectrum would be fully paid for by the higher payments from those on the upper end of the income ladder due to no income cap, even with the lower percentage rates overall. In turn, everyone pays less than under the current tax structure, even with the cap removed from the Social Security tax, as has been suggested. Furthermore, it reduces taxes for employers and for workers, due to the lower tax paid individually through FICA, reduces the penalty for self-employed workers through SECA, and increases the purchasing power for all workers while fully funding the system through an increased revenue base.

The goal is to improve the overall state of the economy, encourage positive wage growth in all levels of the income spectrum, and thus to increase overall revenues for these entitlement programs. Adjustments to these percentages can be made if needed at a later time, but this graduated system will more than adequately fund these programs.

Estate Taxes

Estate taxes are, essentially, a tax on your estate as it passes to children or others after your death. A death tax. Quite literally, it is a tax on your property because of your death. Had you continued to live forever, the tax would have been moot. Thus, the real purpose of the tax on one's estate is to reduce the amount of wealth moving forward to the next generation. Given that the entire purpose of this new tax structure (as well as many of the ideas in this book) is to encourage generational wealth growth for all Americans at all income levels, the idea of a tax on estates is ridiculous. Thus, rather than encourage creative loopholes or other means by which some individuals can circumvent paying a tax on their estate, it is easier to do away with it altogether. No estate taxes for Americans. Let us encourage generational wealth that we can pass along to our families and extended families so future generations have a better starting position in life than we did. Is that not the goal of all families? The Government should not be working against this, and neither should our tax code.

Capital Gains Taxes

Capital gains taxes are a particular category of tax that many Americans have most likely heard of but few understand well, unless they have had to pay them. Essentially, in its simplest explanation, capital gains taxes are paid for gains from the sale of stocks, bonds, some commodities, and real property. Suppose you bought a building at one value, then sold it at another (higher) value, you would have a capital gain. Just as with gains, there can also be losses. For individuals with extensive portfolios of several of these types of assets, they can experience both gains and losses simultaneously. Taxing capital gains is not entirely a negative, but if the taxes are extreme, then it can have a negative effect on investments that may result in these gains. So, the proper balance must be maintained of appropriate taxes on these gains, while also allowing appropriate deductions for losses.

Currently, there are many different ways for individuals who realize a capital gain (meaning that their gains are greater than their losses) to either defer having to pay capital gains taxes or avoid them entirely. Of these mechanisms, seven stand out as being worthwhile. I will briefly mention each of these seven, and why they should remain a part of the proposed new tax code.

First, let's discuss the charitable trust. If you turn over part of your gains to a charity, you should not pay tax on that gain. Makes sense to me, as the charitable organization is likely to use those funds for social benefit. This is a good thing, and one that should be encouraged. Next, the Installment Sale, Deferred Sales Trust, and the Self-Directed Installment Sale. In these cases, an individual accepts payments for an asset, let's say a building, over time. The structuring of these payments would allow deferred payment of capital gains until the final payment is made. Sufficient and this works. The tax gets paid, just deferred until the payments are concluded.

The structured sale is similar to the previously mentioned three (Installment Sale, Deferred Sales Trust, and Self-Directed Installment Sale) in that it allows payments over time, however, in this case, the payments are from an annuity. It is a special case of an In-

stallment Sale. Suppose that you are downsizing your home or retiring from the business you own, for example, and you want to sell
them but want to have the revenue as a guaranteed stream for the
remainder of your life. In this case, the structured sale works well. As
the payments from the annuity are treated as payments in an Installment Sale, there is no reason to remove this type of deferment either.

Lastly, there are the Roth IRA and the primary residence provisions of capital gains taxes. In this case, the capital gains from
within the IRA itself are exempt and up to $250,000 (or $500,000
for married couples) or a personal residence would be exempted from capital gains taxes. I see no reason to change either, as a
change to these two exemptions would not substantially show
any gains in any other area in terms of revenue or public benefit.

That leaves us with three particular changes that should be
made before percentages are even discussed. First, an end to the
process known as Tax Loss Harvesting. What this means is you
deliberately sell assets at a loss so that you can use those losses to
offset gains at some later time in the future. The issue with this is
that it is, essentially, a deliberate attempt at evading capital gains
taxes. To eliminate this procedure, losses taken would need to be
used within the next calendar year or the current calendar year
to offset gains in that year or they would expire. This would affect both individuals and corporations equally. No carrying over
of losses for multiple years into the future. The focus must be on
making good investments, not the strategic use of losses to evade
taxes. Tax loss harvesting is simply a vehicle for tax evasion.

To ensure that gains and losses are measured accurately, gains
should be made using the rate of inflation as a measure. Estimate the
original valuation of the property or asset in today's dollars using
that measure to determine if there was a gain or a loss over the duration of the ownership of the asset. In this way, illusory (deceptive)

gains will be avoided, likewise with illusory losses. Although, the real issue here are gains that are strictly an illusion due to inflation and were not actually gains, but really losses. We want the tax code to be fair and honest, and so too it must be for capital gains taxes as well.

Lastly, there is a particular type of transaction that I did not mention in the list of those to be retained, and that is what is called a 1031 exchange. 1031 exchanges, in the most basic terms are "like-for-like" exchanges, and they should be removed from the tax code. You trade me one asset and I trade you another asset of a like type. You may pay some additional monies, called boot, but in the end, it exchanges assets between us. The concept seems rather benign, but there is an additional caveat. This type of exchange avoids capital gains taxes forever. Yes, forever. For that reason alone, this type of exchange should be removed from the tax code. If individuals or business are making transactions, like for like or not, and a gain is realized, then that gain should be subject to tax. Dividends and other assets are, and so too should these.

Moving to the actual tax rates for capital gains, as with all income tax programs, we again will use a graduated tax structure. However, in this case, the tax rate for capital gains, other than dividends (which would be treated as ordinary income, not capital gains), is not based on your income but how long you hold the asset. This tax system allows for two types of gains – short-term and long-term. Short-term transactions are inherently short, the duration that one holds the asset here is critical. If an asset it held less than six months, or in this case, a very-short-term asset, the tax rate for capital gains on that asset would be the ordinary income tax rate plus 50%. A hefty tax to be sure. However, the intention here is to encourage longer-term investments and these extreme short-term investments by their nature do not do this. If the asset is held longer than six months but less than one year, the rate drops to the ordinary income tax rate plus

25%. Again, a hefty tax, but it is lower than the extreme short-term rate and again is intended to encourage longer term investments.

After the asset has been held for one year and one day, it becomes a long-term asset. At this point, the tax rate on the investment follows a declining rate schedule based on how long the asset has been held. Hold it one year and one day and sell it, realize a gain, and the tax is the ordinary income tax rate plus 15%. Two years and one day of holding that asset reduces the rate to the ordinary income tax rate plus 10%, three years, the capital gains tax falls to the ordinary income tax rate plus 5%. The rate drops by 5% for each interval thereafter as well: 5 years, 10 years, 15 years, and 20 years. At 20 years, the tax reaches its floor, of either zero (at an ordinary income tax rate up to 15%) 5% (for those whose income tax rate is 20%), 10% (for an income tax rate of 25%), and lastly 15% for those whose income tax rate is 30%. The key is the time the asset is held. Hold an asset longer and the tax on it decreases.

Some assets would be exempt from capital gains taxes. In essence, these investments (assets) are guaranteed to make gains. These are U.S. Savings Bonds, Infrastructure Bonds, and Debt Bonds. As discussed before, these are investments in America and its future. As the purchase of these is already credited for tax purposes, and exempt from income taxes when they are redeemed so it makes no sense to tax individuals on the other side (capital gains) when they cash them in after their 20-year term. Other bonds, such as state and municipal bonds, could also be added to this exemption.

Asset Held	**Tax Rate**
< 6 Months	Income Rate + 50%
6 Months - 1 Year	Income Rate + 25%
1 Year + 1 Day	Income Rate + 15%
2 Years + 1 Day	Income Rate + 10%

Asset Held	**Tax Rate**
3 Years + 1 Day	Income Rate + 5%
5 Years + 1 Day	Income Rate + 0%
10 Years + 1 Day	Income Rate - 5%
15 Years + 1 Day	Income Rate - 10%
20 Years	Income Rate - 15%

At 20 years, no further reductions.
So, if the ordinary income tax rate = 15%, at 20 years tax = $0

How does this compare to the current system? Well, for short term assets, the rate is higher – significantly higher for extremely short term assets. When combined with the alternative income tax system discussed above, the tax rate is lower for those assets held by individuals in the highest tax brackets on assets held for at least three to five years.

Corporate Taxes

To truly change how we see taxes, and corporate taxes, we must change what we consider as income. Given that at the present we are taxing both corporations (and their income, which is technically revenue and profit – as well as providing breaks for losses or certain investment behavior) and individuals, our current system is attempting to gain revenue from both sides of this equation. The unfortunate effect that this produces is additional, hidden, tax burdens on individual workers and on consumers. This is done through the reduction in real wages, (even if nominal wages go up), as well as the cutting of benefits, retirement, and passing along of taxes to consumers through higher prices. Let us remember that even though individual employees may receive a "raise" for the year, if the dollar amount of that pay increase is lower than the increase in prices due to inflation and other factors, then what these employees have actually received is a pay cut. This is the difference between what are called real wages and nominal wages. The nominal value is the pre-inflation value of the wages, for example, $8 per hour. The difference with real wages is the value of that $8 over time. So, if a worker continues earning the same wage, $8 per hour, year after year, while inflation rises each year by anything above zero, the worker takes a cut each subsequent year they remain at the same wage. The reason why that is true is because of the change in the purchasing power of that $8 per hour. If the price of a loaf of bread increases each year from $1 to $1.20 to $1.45 and so forth, with the worker still earning the same $8, then they can afford less bread each year after the first.

How does this relate to corporate taxes? If we tax corporate earnings, as well as taxing worker and investor earnings, then we are essentially double-penalizing (or triple-penalizing) the workers for these businesses. They absorb the costs of the taxes through reduced real wages, and increased prices for goods. The response to this should not be to penalize the businesses for shifting the burden onto the consumer and to the worker, as vile as that might be. No, the problem lies with the tax system itself that necessitates such shifting in the first place. If we want to resolve the problem, and we need to, then we must change how we see corporate taxes.

It is true, as others have noted, that the current tax rate for corporate taxes in the United States is one of the highest in the world. It is also true that there are corporations that use the loopholes in the code to essentially reduce their real tax burden to zero while continuing to offshore and shelter earnings in more favorable jurisdictions. Again, the solution here is not punitive penalties to these enterprises, as enticing as it might be, but instead to remedy the reason why these businesses do this in the first place. The same goes for offshoring of manufacturing facilities, customer service, and the lack of care for the end-consumer. In all of these cases, we need to change the environment for business in the United States so that we can demand of our businesses better service, more jobs, and better work environments and wages for our employees.

So, how do we do it? The primary means by which this can be done is simple. Eliminate the corporate tax altogether. This seems radical and slightly counterproductive given that it appears on the surface to be a reward to corporations for their actions in sheltering assets and income, and pundits on both sides will either scream in favor of or against such an idea. What we, as Americans, need to do is to put aside the talking heads and look at what the real effect would be on all of us. In real terms, we need to understand that corporations do not actually pay taxes. We as consumers and as employees pay these taxes since they are passed onto us in the form of lower wages and higher prices. No change to the rate will solve the problem, as it is still a hidden tax on workers and consumers. Only full abolition of the corporate tax will solve the problem.

Consumption Taxes and the FairTax

Consumption taxes function wholly different from income taxes in that they do not tax individuals for working or saving. In fact, they tax individuals only when and how they choose to consume. In this case, they operate more efficiently and effectively as taxes on both earnings and wealth than an income tax. Suppose that individuals opt to save their income, consuming nearly nothing, for most of their life. They then pass along that vast wealth to their children, who then use it to purchase items for themselves or others. The individual who opted to save the money paid little in tax, but the children who opted to spend portions of the wealth then paid taxes on that wealth through their consumption. This is the basic idea behind consumption taxes, and they can, and do, produce adequate operational revenues in lieu of direct income taxes, without the negative effects on wages, consumption, and savings produced by income taxes.

The FairTax

The FairTax is a plan designed by the organization called American for Fair Taxation, and is designed as a consumption, or sales, tax on new goods or services only. They propose a national consumption tax at a rate of 23%, with the added caveat of a prebate (or a rebate on taxes paid before they are paid, to make the tax progressive and provide the needed tax relief for those below the poverty line). The tax is designed only to be charged for new products and services, which means that used goods are exempt from tax. This opens up a host of new ideas for a strengthened market for used products.

Furthermore, the tax, at 23% is revenue neutral, meaning that the revenue generated would cover the current expenses for all of our governmental programs, such as Medicare and Social Security. However, the key thing to remember in this is that the FairTax is designed to wholly replace a score of different taxes we currently pay, meaning that those taxes would cease to exist. Federal Income Taxes would be abolished, along with corporate taxes, alternative minimum taxes, capital gains taxes, estate (or death) taxes, gifts taxes, and FICA/SECA taxes. In turn, the IRS is eliminated and individuals take their entire paycheck home as income.

One example that I have used to explain the difference between a consumption tax, such as the FairTax, and income taxes is this. First, suppose that you earn $1,500 on your paycheck. As the government, I will take my $525 (or 35% for this example), leaving you with

$975. Now, you go to the store and decide to buy groceries. The total for your grocery bill is $214 (assuming 7% local sales taxes), leaving you less than $761 to pay all other expenses this period. Now let's assume instead that there were no income tax, but simply a consumption tax on new goods. Let's also assume for this example, that you are above the eligibility for the prebate. You earn the same $1,500, but since there are no income taxes, you keep all of what you earned. You then go to buy groceries, which now, after the FairTax is added, cost $260 (23% FairTax, 7% local sales taxes). This leaves you with $1,240 left for all other expenses and you have paid, rather than $525 in taxes, a total thus far of $46 in tax. The more you spend in that month the more tax you would pay, obviously, but it links with consumer spending for new goods, not a penalty because you earned income.

	Initial Income	Income Tax	Take-Home	Food Expense*	Sales Tax	Money Left
Current System	$1,500	$525	$975	$214	7%	$761
Fair Tax	$1,500	$0	$1,500	$260	30%	$1,240

Food expense includes sales tax paid.

After describing the two scenarios, I asked various individuals in which case they felt better about their financial situation. In every case, they cited that the second scenario made them feel better since they got to take all of their money home upfront and then spend it how they felt was best for their situation. They would pay their taxes when they opted to consume, not because they were employed. For those who were self-employed, the response was even more in favor of the second scenario, since they get hit harder on taxes due to penalties for errors in quarterly filings (which do happen), the additional taxes paid out of their income due to being classified as "self-employed" courtesy of SECA taxes, and also, in some cases, paying the Alternative Minimum Tax.

The only area where I differ from the FairTax proposal in terms of my own view, is with respect to capital gains taxes. I understand that if you tax capital gains that you are inherently taxing income, as it is income from investments. However, I believe that if individuals were encouraged to make investments for the long term (such as venture capital, long-term research and development, etc.), entrepreneurialism will benefit. We need a whole new generation of entrepreneurs to emerge, but they will need funding for their ventures to become successes, employing the countless millions of Americans who seek work today and will seek work in the future. To realize our true potential for the future, we must ensure that these long term investments are encouraged.

Is this social engineering? Perhaps to a degree. However, on the whole, a modest tax on short term investments would likely produce the desired effect without burdensome regulations. All that would be required for those who claim a capital gain (or loss) would be to file a short form denoting the income (or losses) from investments and business ventures that year. Apply a tax rate based on the time the asset has been held (if there was a gain and you realized the gain by cashing out your asset, essentially, in this case) and there is the amount due. One check, once a year, and you can carry over losses from the previous year for one year. So, if I lost money this year, I can claim that loss next year.

For those individuals who are willing to look beyond the confines of income taxes, the FairTax is a viable, workable, and good choice for an alternative tax system, compared with the failed system we presently have in place. If we want true tax equality, then we must tax consumption not income. There is no reason that the individual who bought a yacht should pay less, by percentage, in tax than the individual working at a restaurant waiting tables, or the worker mopping floors at the local school. It should not happen, but it does in the current system. True tax equality comes only when we stop looking at employment and income as a means to fund our government, and when we stop looking at Americans as criminals for their ignorance of the 70,000 pages of tax policy that they will likely never read, nor understand given the ridiculously complicated nature of the current tax code.

No Corporate Taxes

Given that corporations don't pay taxes, the FairTax also abolishes corporate taxes. Furthermore, we should abolish taxes such as "sin" taxes, on alcohol and tobacco, and abolish "use" taxes, such as taxes on gasoline, which constitute a significant portion of our price at the pump. If we eliminate these taxes, all of which are essentially "sin" taxes, we can achieve a fairer, equitable tax system. Employ the FairTax on all new products, whether it be a gallon of gasoline or a new pair of shoes or even that new yacht. Taxes paid on the yacht will obviously be higher than on that pair of shoes, but that is only fair.

A whole new market emerges

Since the FairTax targets only new sales, it exempts secondary markets entirely. This has the potential to create a whole new market for used products. Instead of disposable products, Americans could again enjoy the use of products which have a longer life expectancy than a few months or a year. Instead of purchasing an item that breaks in six months, we could encourage production of items (even if at a higher initial price) that would allow us the option to sell the item to another individual later, allowing them to enjoy its use, recouping our taxes paid and exempting the second buyer from paying tax at all.

The possibilities are endless for the number of new jobs and new market possibilities that this opens up. Only through the abolition of income taxes and the institution of a consumption tax, such as the FairTax, can we achieve this sort of explosive market growth and encourage a thriving entrepreneurialism to create newer, more durable, products that best facilitate stronger, more vibrant brands, and allow for resale to future users. These users, in turn, will become more likely to purchase new items from these more-durable brands, thus increasing tax revenues in the long run. This increases brand loyalty (for those brands willing to produce these sorts of products) and reinforces the need to produce quality products here in the United States with our technological skill and advanced manufacturing capabilities.

What is a "prebate" anyway?

One area in which individuals commonly misunderstand the FairTax and how it differs from other consumption or sales taxes, is with respect to the prebate. I briefly mentioned this in my earlier general discussion of the FairTax. A prebate, generally speaking, is a payment to a consumer before they make purchases that covers estimated tax expenses for a given month. The prebate would be a payment BEFORE you bought something, paying you upfront to cover the cost of the taxes you pay when you shop. This differs from a rebate as it is something received after you spend. Prebate, using the prefix "pre," designates this payment comes upfront, before the purchase is made. The prebate is a payment upfront to cover what it is anticipated that you, as a consumer, would spend in tax payments that month from purchases.

As I said previously, without any prebate mechanism, consumption taxes are inherently regressive. When you factor in the prebate, however, the FairTax becomes progressive at all levels of income, negating the taxes paid by those who need the assistance the most: the poor. If we expected someone who was paid $8.00 per hour to pay the same in tax, by percentage, as someone who earned $50 million in a given year, we would be laying a disproportionate burden on the one earning less, for whom taxes on purchases is far more damaging. The prebate removes that issue by ensuring that those who are around the poverty line are not punished for spending, and for doing their part in our consumer-driven economy.

Still confused as to what a prebate is? Think of it this way – you go to a store and you buy a new TV. The TV costs you $2,000, but they tell you that if you mail in your receipt you will receive a check for $500 as a rebate, making the price of the TV now $1,500. However, for the time between your purchase, where you paid the whole $2,000 and the time the check arrives for your $500 rebate, you have lost the use of that $500. With a prebate, you would instead see the price of the TV as $2,000, but now, instead of sending you a check later, you receive the check for the $500 upfront, so even though you pay $2,000 at the register, you really only paid $1,500, and did not lose your use of the remaining $500 waiting for a check in the mail to reimburse you. The prebate puts that money in your hand before you even go to the store to shop in the first place.

Does this mean some individuals will certainly have the option to spend less and pocket the balance of the prebate as savings? Sure, but in the end, what is the problem here? We should encourage saving even by those whose financial means are the smallest and thus improve their financial position over time, including for future generations.

Joshua R. Yates

Joshua R. Yates

Entitlement Reform

Beyond the protections enshrined within the Constitution, are we truly "entitled" to anything from our government? Instead of "entitlements," the appropriate phrase we should be using is "social safety net." Social Security, Medicare, Medicaid, unemployment benefits, housing assistance programs, among other forms of government assistance are all examples of "social safety net" programs. Some people may never have need of the programs in the social safety net; others will require assistance several times in their lives. This is the essence of these programs. Nearly every American will utilize at least one of these programs at some point in their lives. As with many things, there are individuals who are adamantly opposed to social safety net programs, at least, until they need them or somehow benefit from them. Because these programs always produce such visceral responses (either from those supporting or opposing them) it often seems as though it is impossible to effectively make any changes to these programs. Any change that is made is bound to anger someone, somewhere, and so the best political option is often to do nothing at all. That is simply not good enough anymore, we must make needed changes, we cannot afford to put the decisions off to the future any longer.

Just to be clear, I do not advocate elimination or a dismantling of the social safety net. However, I am a realist in the fact that changes are needed to strengthen these programs today and keep

75

them solvent for the future. This does not mean that additional changes might not be needed again in the future; the decision on those changes, however, rests with future generations so that they can develop solutions that address their relevant and contemporary needs. What we can do now, however, is to reform these programs for our nation today, and for the current and next generation's needs.

The Social Safety Net: Do we need it?

There is an ongoing debate as to if we should even have a government-supported social safety net at all, with some claiming that these programs are best done by charities (such as religious groups and non-profit organizations) and others claiming that private charities are incapable of handling the load. Additionally, it is also stated that the social safety net creates an entitlement society which is lazy, and that these programs induce people to become lazy and to not seek to better themselves, preferring to live off of the government. It is with this third group that I vehemently disagree.

While there are some individuals who abuse the system and who truly wish to live off of the government, these are the anomaly. We all hear the stories of the individuals who live in million dollar homes and collect "welfare and food stamps" but I cannot say strongly enough that these are not the norm. The problem with our system is not that we have a social safety net, but that it is ineffective in countering some of the social and economic forces that it exists to prevent or overcome. For example, if an individual is in enough financial hardship as to qualify for most government aid, they are effectively discouraged from working additional jobs as doing so would raise their income just enough that they would likely be disqualified for further assistance, but not enough income to overcome their current financial hardship. The issue here is not that don't we want people off of government assistance; we do, but that the income from working one or two additional jobs is often just not enough to offset the loss of the government aid. In this case, the issue is not that the individuals do not want to work; it is that if they work, the benefits of working are outweighed by the loss in aid to help them to overcome the hardship of poverty and break free from it forever. Better would be to continue the aid until the individual was able to support themselves on their own financially, through sufficient income, within a reasonable amount of time. What is a reasonable amount of time? That should be discussed, but for me, no more than two years seems reasonable. Let's remember, the social safety net is meant to be temporary assistance, not a permanent means of support. The goal is to assist those individuals who need a little help in the short term, not to make use of the safety net a way of life.

The system is not designed to tell individuals what they can or cannot spend their income on, nor should it. Having a government program or bureaucrat determine that having items like "a car" or "a TV" is somehow indicative of poor spending choices is simply arbitrary and inappropriate. Anyone of us could purchase those items for fairly low prices, including sales and buying used. Instead of some veiled attempt at social engineering, the goal should be simply increasing real income and wages. It is counterproductive to punish an individual for attempting to improve themselves to end their reliance on government aid.

As wages have remained largely stagnant, or in some cases declined, over the past few decades (real wages - wages adjusted for price increases and inflation, rather than nominal - the face value of the pay in dollars, not adjusted for inflation or other expenses), costs for food, fuel, transportation, medical care, and other necessities have continually increased. The reality is that our society requires a social safety net. To abandon these individuals, with claims that their financial problems are their own fault and they need to pay the price, is callous and just frankly un-American in my mind. Americans stand with one another, we take care of each other when we are down or hurting, and we work to better each other through our communities. It is what makes us strong, it is what makes our nation endure, and it is why we need a social safety net.

Reforming "Welfare" and Unemployment

Our current welfare system, decentralized to the states, has not worked to end the issue of poverty within our nation. States have historically had a mixed ability to address the problem of poverty on the same scale as the federal government. This is not a case where one state is simply better at eliminating poverty than another, nor is it an issue of states being not up to the task. It is that by leaving the solution to poverty (and therefore the application of social safety net policies) up to the states creates a patchwork solution to combatting poverty which produces artificial and unnecessary disparities between states. Poverty relief should not be relegated only to the states. It should be a universal constant, that a citizen who is impoverished can know that the same aid will be available wherever they are in the country.

In the long run, the solution to poverty is obvious. Rather than continually handing out money or other assistance, the road out of poverty is ultimately through improving economic growth throughout our country, with strong employment options, competitive wages, and people working together in our communities to eliminate poverty forever. Unfortunately, the current design of our "welfare" program encourages individuals not to seek either additional work or increased wages as crossing certain income thresholds reduces aid by a greater amount than the income the individual gained, as we already discussed. Let's keep in mind that until an individual achieves income proportionally higher compared to what they had when they sought aid, it is unlikely that any program will be effective in bringing the individual, or family, out of poverty. Furthermore, our current aid programs are discriminatory based on age and gender. What I mean by this is - if you happen to be female, and have children, the programs available to you outweigh those who have no children, or might be male, with or without small children. It is not unreasonable to believe that an individual might be male and have a small child that they are raising without the mother present. It does happen. Yet, the programs are specifically designed for women with children instead. Even if not openly excluding single fathers who may be raising children on their own - which again does happen - the very name of the programs themselves assume otherwise. These programs need to change, drastically.

The changes that I propose are extensive, but will reform our welfare programs into ones that truly encourage individuals to break the cycle of poverty and to advance themselves. First, we must repeal the Personal Responsibility and Work Opportunity Reconciliation Act of 1996, also known as Public Law 104-193. This would pave the way for a return to federalization of these programs. This means we will need to also terminate the TANF program, as well as the WIC program. While some might find this callous and argue that this will harm children that is not the intention. The goal here is to lift individuals out of poverty, not subsidize it. To do this, we must think about welfare differently. If the parent(s) are gainfully employed and are able to earn a solid wage, it is more likely than not that they will be able to successfully provide for their children. If we fix the real problem, rather than treating the symptoms or effects of poverty, the additional aid will not be needed. However, there is a component that is often forgotten in the fight against poverty, hunger, and homelessness, to name a few: private charities. While we are shifting the way in which we deliver assistance (as will be discussed momentarily), we should address the interim period, which will require the government to work in conjunction with private charities to provide short-term relief while individuals shift to the new system. These private charities are around us already, and while we cannot immediately terminate these existing programs and expect these charities to suddenly carry the additional load, we can work closely with these charities in the interim to provide the resources in anticipation of an increased short-term load. At the same time, the government should work closely with these charities to ensure resources are being delivered where they are needed most, and to help them to integrate individuals they are assisting into the new program to replace the plethora of current "welfare" programs.

As I have said, we need a new system, one system, to replace the institutionalized network of current welfare programs. We need a system which not only encourages, but enables individuals to break the cycle of poverty. To do this, I propose the creation of a new federal WPA-style program to replace traditional welfare, workfare, and unemployment programs. For simplicity, I will simply use the reference of "new WPA" to refer to this program. Do not let this confuse you though; it is not a reincarnation of the WPA (Works Progress Administration) program from the New Deal. I use the acronym simply as a means to illustrate the idea.

In this new WPA program, individuals would be eligible for federal aid in the form of wages, paying the prevailing wage in that region for work done, with wages based on the specific job that an individual does, such as maintenance, roadwork, clerical, and so forth. For individuals who are already employed, part of what are referred to as the 'working poor' - working, yet either just above or below the poverty line - this program offers an opportunity for additional income, but more importantly, the program would offer free training programs for particular industries. Done in conjunction with universities, community colleges, technical colleges, corporations, and labor unions, for example, this new WPA program would help individuals to acquire skills in particular industries, while working, and then help them to find permanent employment in the private sector in that field, thus leaving the program. This should increase their income, but more importantly, would allow them to transition out of the need for the social safety net. Their wages and benefits (from the program) would continue for a short time after they move to private employment, called the post-transition period, and then terminate.

During this post-transition period, the program would monitor the employee's progress through communication with the individual and also with their new employer, to make sure that they were adjusting appropriately to their new job. This follow-up is necessary to the success of the program, as it helps to ensure a low return rate to the program after an individual has transitioned out. The follow-up also helps to facilitate any changes that might be needed in the program through the communication with participants and employers to be sure that the training received through the program adequately prepared individuals for the jobs they transitioned into, and that the pay in those jobs is sufficient to prevent recidivism onto social safety net programs. Individuals then have a real chance to transcend poverty, employers gain better-prepared employees from the program already trained in relevant and needed skills, and the government is able to remove one more individual from the rolls of the social safety net. This was the original intention, or should have been, of any sort of "welfare" system, and is consistent with the American tradition of self-reliance and individuality, rather than subsistence on government subsidies or handouts.

In addition to skills training and education, as well as job placement assistance, this new WPA would participate in urban and infrastructure renewal projects nationwide. This would allow individuals the opportunity to help rebuild our nation, while also learning useful skills for their future. Furthermore, it ensures that individuals are working for the benefits they earn. As stated earlier, during an individual's time in this program, they would be paid the prevailing wage in their local area. This ensures that individuals are paid according to local factors and are not, therefore, over or underpaid in their region. The program needs to be a viable alternative to help individuals move out of poverty, rather than simply a program where they never leave, nor one where we try and push them out of the system as fast as possible so we can claim we have done a good job, even though they are still chronically impoverished. For the program to be successful, we need to ensure that the employers are active participants in the program, helping to ensure that the skills training, or retraining in some cases, is aligned with current regional industry needs and thus provides them with good, quality employees for their businesses.

The program is not only intended for those who are in poverty, but could also be extended to be an alternative to unemployment benefits as well. Given that this program offers benefits as wages, offers training (or retraining), and helps with job placement, it is a feasible alternative for those who are among the long-term unemployed or underemployed. There is no reason that many of the jobs within the agency administering the program, at least at the local level, could not be done by the individuals participating in the program. This is to say that many of the clerks and office staff could also be individuals working in the program. The American workforce is not entirely industrial or clerical and this program must also reflect that. In this way, rather than cash handouts for unemployment, the program would help to return the unemployed back to the workforce once again.

State governments understand local and regional employment needs better than a purely federal agency, and so this new WPA program should be jointly administered by the states. That reduces redundancies between state and federal unemployment initiatives and helps to share the burden universally. By including states in the program as joint administrators, it allows innovations that might be created in one state to filter to others, improving the program everywhere. Also, by combining welfare, workfare, and unemployment into the same program, it allows for the program to be effectively branded as a work program, not just a program for the unemployed and not just for the poor or working poor. It shifts from being "welfare" to being an economic improvement program, working for all of us, individual and business alike.

Obviously a limit would need to be established for how long an individual could work in the program, but that would need to be determined at a later time. What is important now is not determining how long people could remain in the program, but rather, what we want the program to do and how it can reduce costs in the long run as well as reducing the number of Americans that are living in poverty or have been unemployed for an extended period of time, many of which have simply given up trying to find employment due to a wide variety of factors. The overall goal in this is to retain a social safety net, but to ensure that individuals are working for benefits, as well as helping them to better themselves and their employment options so that they will not need these programs in the future.

Poverty is the enemy, and it must be fought directly, regardless of how an individual ended up impoverished, how long they have been impoverished, or what their background is. What matters is that we are ready to step up and do our part if others are willing to do theirs. In the end, everyone benefits. They earn wages, allowing them to spend, which results in taxes. We rebuild our infrastructure.

Individuals have the opportunity to retrain or simply take advantage of the job placement services in exchange for their work time. Their incomes increase, allowing them to better care for themselves and their family. The potential for abuse is minimized as individuals work for benefits, rather than any sort of direct cash payment or benefit card. Also, the inclusion of local businesses, as well as labor unions and educational institutions helps to fully integrate the program and its participants into their communities, and to help them reach for a new future - one without poverty. Given the current economic situation, it is likely that the program would be heavily utilized at this point, but that would likely taper off over time as the economy improves and more people find employment either on their own or through the program. As the services are less needed, costs will drop further. Therefore, it must be accepted that this program's financial needs should reflect the current economic situation. The worse our economic state as a society, the higher its funding needs will be. The better our economic situation as a whole, the lower the program's funding needs will be. It must remain flexible, and adapt to the situation at the moment, as should all government programs.

Social Security

Social Security is one of our nation's most widely known, and longest-lasting, social safety net programs. Created to ensure the our nation never had a repeat of the mass poverty among our older citizens, as was experienced during the Great Depression, the main focus of the program has continued largely unchanged through to today. However, demographics change and today our nation's oldest citizens live longer lives than previously. With the pending retirements of the Baby Boomer generation, arguably the largest generation in recent American history, the financial solvency of the program is questioned. This said, looking at the tax revenue from FICA and SECA show that for years to come, the program still has excess revenue well beyond its projected needs.

Several questions come to mind when discussing any changes in Social Security or its solvency in the future. First, what about the decline in the number of people in the workforce, leading to potentially lower revenue from FICA and SECA taxes, as the Baby Boomers retire? To answer this question, we need to look at what is suggested by the retirement of the "boomers" and the effect on tax revenue. In other words, the idea here is that the size of the pie (or total tax revenue) will dramatically shrink in a short time span. However, the idea that tax revenue will make a rapid decline as the "boomers" retire is a fallacy. With a growing population from both births and immigration, America will keep a strong, productive workforce for the foreseeable future. Sure, there are a vast number of individuals who will retire in the next twenty years, but we simply cannot discount population growth (and new immigration) during that same time span.

Unlike some countries in Europe, the population growth rate of the United States is not negative. We are growing, just slowly. This growth and the resulting number of people entering the workforce as a result, the size of the revenue pie (total tax revenue collected from FICA/SECA taxes) will continue to grow. The ratio of working-to-retired is not where we need to focus, it is a red herring. Instead, our goal should be to grow the total size of the pie through increasing incomes of all Americans and reducing unemployment nationwide, rather than focusing on divvying up a supposedly shrinking pie. When Americans are prosperous as a whole people, with steady, reliable incomes that allow them to provide for themselves and their families (including saving for the future), sufficient tax revenues will exist. If we had a tax system, such as the Fair-

Tax, coupled with strong, prosperous citizens, earning solid incomes with livable wages, they would be consuming, thus providing the needed tax revenue. Increasing incomes and reducing unemployment are two areas of utmost importance to Social Security solvency.

Second, retirement by Baby Boomers will be slow and gradual, not all at once. Therefore, the "shocks" of declining tax revenue and rapid increases in the number of individuals drawing from the system are not truly shocks at all, but can be planned for and anticipated in advance. Remember, for each "boomer" who retires, there will be new individuals entering and advancing in the workforce. The focus cannot, and must not, be on how many "boomers" are retiring. It must be on maintaining a strong workforce filled with a new generation of Americans. Focusing in this will ensure the adequate revenues, regardless of how many "boomers" begin drawing from the system. Again, a consumption tax like the FairTax would alleviate much of this worry outright. All of these numbers that we are worrying about are based on revenue generated by income taxes. Shifting to a consumption tax would remedy the issue outright, keeping income in the hands of those who earned it, boosting consumption, while still providing the revenue needed to fund Social Security for the foreseeable future.

So, knowing that the increase in recipients is going to be gradual and revenue will not evaporate overnight causing Social Security to run out of money immediately, where is the problem? Social Security has one glaring issue with its future financial solvency. That issue is that revenue collected under FICA and SECA taxes for Social Security is being shifted to "general revenue" in government budgets. Any solution to Social Security and its solvency must first address this problem. If we are spending tax money collected for Social Security on everything except Social Security, we cannot claim that Social Security is out of money. The issue is not with Social Security, but instead with the fact we spent the money on things OTHER than Social Security.

How social security funds are "shifted" to general revenue

When we (both individuals and employers) pay our FICA (and SECA, in the case of the self-employed) taxes, the largest portion is the Social Security tax. These tax funds, once they are collected by the government, are then converted by the U.S. Treasury into what are called "special issue" securities, which generate interest. They are effectively a special kind of government bond. What happens to your Social Security taxes after they are converted into these bonds? The money that you paid in taxes for Social Security is then used as general revenue by the government. Essentially, the taxes you paid toward Social Security instead paid for other expenditures (but not Social Security) on the promise that the government will repay itself later when Social Security benefits need to be paid. As with any government-issued bond, if the government defaults, we are left with nothing. At its most basic, Social Security operates as a system of I.O.U.s from one part of the government to another, even though we pay taxes that are supposed to fund it.

Through this convoluted financing structure, Social Security operates with very little actual cash on-hand, only ever having enough money to pay current benefits at any given time. Additionally, these "special issue" bonds are government debt, owed by one part of the government to another, the debt owed to Social Security comprises part of the national debt. Because this financing scheme uses Social Security tax money to fund general expenditures by the government, it masks the true severity of government deficits. Without the massive infusion of these Social Security tax dollars in general revenue (effectively becoming a "double inclusion" in the budget, even as they appear earmarked for social security), the deficits the government currently runs would be substantially higher. Social Security, however, would be fully funded. Even though revenues for social security are automatically converted into these special bonds, the taxes collected for Social Security appear on the budget as being derived from FICA/SECA (and even says it was from the Social Security tax, giving the impression of those funds going into a separate Social Security pool), but in reality they are treated as just another source of general revenue funds, just like your federal income taxes.

Confused? Don't be. A great deal of the nearly all government budgets are purposefully designed to be confusing if you aren't familiar with the terminology they use. This example should help explain how it works. When you pay taxes, you provide revenue for the government. What the taxes were paid for (in this case, Social Security) determines what is done with that money when the government receives it.

To keep it simple, let's consider "general revenue" to be a big pile of money that the government uses to pay various non-specific expenses. It might pave streets, pay salaries, or buy a squadron of fighter aircraft, as examples. Social security, however, doesn't draw from general revenue. Because of how it was designed, it has its own separate pile, but not of money. It has a big pile of bonds, essentially a giant pile of I.O.U. slips. When your Social Security tax money comes in, the government hands it to the Treasury, who then hands the government a bond. The government then puts their new bond on the separate Social Security pile while the Treasury puts the tax money that they exchanged the bond for (taxes collected for Social Security) onto the big pile of money for general revenue spending.

When money is needed to pay out social security benefits, the government goes to its stack of bonds, picks up enough to cover however much it needs to pay out in Social Security benefits at the time, and goes to the Treasury to "cash in" the bonds for their expected face value. The Treasury will then either take that money from the general revenue pile or simply issue new additional debt to pay for the old debt (a process known as debt rolling). If this looks like a shells game with large sums of money to you, then you aren't alone.

This is one of the reasons that people question why Social Security is funding the rest of the government, since it provides nearly half of all federal income tax revenues. In fiscal year 2010 (FY 2010), Social Security taxes alone were $631.7 billion. Medicare taxes were $233.1 billion, for a total in payroll FICA/SECA taxes of $864.8 billion. Compare that to federal income taxes, which brought in only $898.5 billion in revenue, and those two (personal income taxes and payroll - FICA/SECA combined - taxes) are the two largest revenue items in the entire federal budget. All others streams of revenue, including corporate income taxes (which are really paid by consumers), produced less total revenue combined than the revenue from the Medicare portion of FICA/SECA taxes by itself.

It is time we get serious about government spending, and about where our tax monies go. When we pay a tax, we should expect (and demand) that the government spend those dollars exactly as they have said they would. Every dollar taken from people in taxes is a dollar they do not have to spend on their own family's needs. It is shameful that this government shells game has gone on this long, and it is time that we do something to change it, starting with reforming Social Security to ensure its solvency today and for the future.

Reforming Social Security

Most calls to reform Social Security either call for a privatization plan (which has been tried in other countries, and was so unsuccessful that it was abandoned) or advocate for an increase in the age at which individuals are eligible to receive benefits. The issue with both approaches is that both of these approaches do not get at the heart of the issue facing Social Security, which is its financial solvency in the long-term, nor do they provide a reasonable alternative to the current status-quo with respect to our social safety net.

The fact of the matter is that we simply cannot abolish Social Security and replace it with a private savings plan. Such a privatization plan would disrupt the federal revenue shells game currently in place. If the government simply mandated that you put a certain percentage of your income into a private savings plan, rather than paying taxes to fund social security, it would be the same as effectively cutting federal revenues in half. Privatization plans are all talk with no substance. No member of Congress would ever vote for a reform that would gut federal revenues, as they know that such a plan would bring to light the dirty side of deficits and a likely produce an even greater amount of debt spending. Even more, if the private savings plans were voluntary then it would gut the social safety net as it exists today, and we would run the risk of returning to a society where our older citizens potentially could be impoverished. Other countries have attempted private savings plans as alternatives to a social security system, and those attempts universally have failed. We cannot afford to gamble with the future, we need stability. Social safety net programs, such as Social Security, attempted to resolve an issue within our society that we faced during the Great Depression and is still with us today.

The second often proposed solution, raising the retirement age, is equally dubious in resolving the issues facing Social Security. If we raise the retirement age then we can safely assume that means that most Americans will remain in the workforce longer. However, with so many Americans working longer anyway, is this a problem? From my perspective, it is. Our society, as it is currently structured, is based around the idea that new workers enter the workforce at a young age, bringing with them new ideas, new education, and new viewpoints. These, in turn, help reshape the workplace (slowly) and allow new knowledge brought by these new workers to improve our businesses. Social Security, and retirement in general, provided an impetus for older workers to leave the workforce at relatively younger ages (62-65) and to actually enjoy retirement while they were still able to do so. Their departure from the workforce provided opportunities for newer workers to advance, succeeding these newly retired workers, and thus even newer workers would enter the workforce in turn.

However, if these older workers remain in the workforce longer, then our entire societal paradigm would change. Advancement in careers would be slowed, older workers would remain longer and the diffusion of new knowledge would be slowed. This is not meant to be a condemnation of older workers. Far from it. The trade-off in experience and knowledge of the job for new information and less experience is one that must be determined on an individual basis by individual businesses. The point is, if we increase the age for benefits to be drawn, we reduce the incentive for workers who had considered retirement to do so.

The first thing that we need to do is to stop the shells game with Social Security tax money. We can do this by requiring, as we have done with Medicare taxes, that Social Security tax money cannot be used to fund anything other than Social Security. That means no more special bonds, no more debt rolling to pay Social Security, no more bonanza of revenue for general expenditures. Some people call this a "lock box" and the analogy is fairly straightforward. We pay taxes to fund Social Security, that money should go right back out to pay benefits.

Next, we remove the cap on income for FICA and SECA taxes. Yes, that means that you would be paying those taxes on all of your income, from all sources. This would likely produce additional revenue from the system and would ensure that high income earners cannot shield the vast bulk of their income from these taxes while the rest of society pays the tax on all of their income.

Additionally, we need to alter the structure for benefits. Remember, Social Security is a social safety net program. It is designed to keep senior citizens out of poverty. It is not intended to be a car payment, second home mortgage payment, or something of that sort. Sure, it doesn't cover all of someone's living expenses, but it's meant to be a support program not full income replacement. Therefore, to be sure that the people getting Social Security are the ones who actually need it, we need to implement a system of means testing, based on income and asset thresholds.

After age 60, and every five years thereafter, individuals would need to report their income and asset valuations for Social Security eligibility. This is not meant to be a long schedule of individually indexed assets, but gross totals in terms of cash values (such as property tax valuations) along with some form of income reporting, such as a tax return or annual pay stubs. The means test index would assume that an individual would retire at age 65, and would expect that an individual would live for 25 years, or through age 90.

Also, in assessing an individual's assets, we would allow for two deductions. First, we allow a home deduction of $250,000. If your home is valued at a higher or lower amount, you still get a deduction of $250,000. The same goes for individuals who rent. Each individual can claim the deduction, and so a couple (combined) would have a deduction of $500,000. This is intended, as asset values for couples (either married or in a civil union) are determined individually. All jointly held assets are split 50/50 between the two for asset calculation purposes. Using the adjusted asset values, the means testing would be fairly straightforward from there.

Individual Total Assets*	Social Security Benefits
$ 1,000,000	100%
$ 1,375,000	75%
$ 1,750,000	50%
$ 2,125,000	25%
$ 2,500,000	0%

After $250,000 Home Ownership Deduction

First, if your combined income and assets at age 60 (since the initial evaluation for age 65 eligibility occurs at age 60) is below $1,000,000, then you are eligible to receive 100% of your earned Social Security benefits. If an individual exceeds $1,375,000 in total income and assets, Social Security benefits drop to 75%. After $1,750,000 the benefits reduce again to 50%, with the benefits falling to 25% after an individual reaches an income and asset total of more than $2,125,000. Once an individual passes $2,500,000 in total income and assets, their Social Security benefits would be zero. They would still be required to pay the taxes, but they would not receive benefits upon retirement. The program's benefits are not designed for them. It is designed to help those less fortunate who need assistance in their retirement years. This declining benefits system, through means testing, would ensure that those who need the benefits get them while preventing Social Security monies from becoming car payments or vacation money for those who don't financially need the benefits from the program. This responsible approach to Social Security, including the removal of the income cap on FICA and SECA taxes as well as the implementation of a "lock box" approach to Social Security tax monies would resolve the financial uncertainty with Social Security and ensure that the program remains solvent for the next generations.

Let's be clear, these changes would need to apply to everyone, not just future recipients. It is wholly unfair to say to one group of people that they're not going to be subject to the same rules as another group. No, the rules must apply equally to all of us, and so that means current Social Security recipients must be included. It is likely that this means some people would lose their benefits, those for whom the program was not intended. However, it is more likely that there would be no change for the vast majority of current recipients and near future recipients. What we want to avoid is a two-tiered system where one group operates under one set of rules and another group operates under a second set of rules. We also must avoid the temptation to have a sort of "phased-in" reform, as this opens the door for the very two-tiered approaches we should be avoiding. Furthermore, phase-ins and two-tiered rules add confusion and uncertainty. Means testing is straightforward, is fair, and is a solution we can implement today. Removing the income cap on FICA and SECA is likewise fair and something we can implement today.

Medicare

Medicare is another staple of our social safety net, charged with providing medical insurance to our older citizens so they are not left without medical care in their retirement. However, this same program is also called "socialized medicine," "single-payer coverage," and "national healthcare" by some, with others going so far as to argue for "Medicare for all" as a solution to the issue of rising healthcare costs, and a lack of medical insurance among a growing number of Americans.

The problem is that none of these characterizations of Medicare are accurate. It is not "socialized medicine" and it is not "single-payer." Coinsurance, and supplemental insurance, as well as out-of-pocket expenses remain, meaning that in any given situation, there might be three or four "payers," certainly more than one. It is not "socialized medicine" to use the generic version of the term, meaning "government-owned, operated, and controlled," as Medicare acts only as insurance, and does not run its own hospitals or pay its own staff physicians to treat patients (although given certain locations and practices, it might as well).

The solution is not simply reform, but rather the ending of the program as it currently exists. I know, some of you reading this might think that this means I intend to abandon senior citizens to private insurance or no insurance, or that I somehow don't see the need and usefulness of Medicare. That is not the case. I simply feel reform, here, is futile. We need to think more radically here, and think bigger. What we need, instead, is true, universal, single-payer health insurance, available to all U.S. citizens.

This is not "socialized medicine"

Let's be clear. When the phrase "socialized medicine" is tossed around, it usually comes with images of the old Soviet Union, communism, big brother, death panels, and the like. Those images are meant to simply scare people away from considering an option that we should consider when it comes to healthcare. What single-payer means is that there is one single payer for all medical expenses. So, you go to the clinic or hospital, see your doctor, and go home. The doctor then submits their claim for payment from that single payer, rather than billing you for some amount, your insurance for another, and so on, with each patient having some different insurer as a payer. These multiple payers increase expenses on medical staff who send claims to different insurers, with those increased costs eventually making their to you in the form of increased premiums, higher deductibles, and more out-of-pocket expenses.

We can have single-payer health insurance without having government-run hospitals and clinics, and without having doctors on the government payroll. There are no death panels, or care rationing (both of which we actually have right now in the current system). Even more, there is still a role for existing insurance companies to play in a single-payer system, as agents and administrators working with the government to operate the single-payer plan regionally.

Why Medicare isn't single-payer

I touched on this briefly earlier, but I feel this needs further explanation to make clear the differences between Medicare (and other insurance), and a single-payer plan. Assume you are a patient, and you have Medicare. Now, when you go to the doctor, and are billed, Medicare pays some of the costs, but you may have a deductible (or some other out-of-pocket portion you have to pay). You might also have supplemental insurance which pays a portion of the costs too. Each of these is a separate payer. Medicare is number one, you are number two, and your supplemental insurance (or coinsurance) is number three. Therefore, this particular visit had three payers, not one. If you have a needed prescription, this may be paid either wholly by the supplemental insurance (single-payer) or jointly by you with some out-of-pocket deductible or co-pay (two payers).

So, in this example we have three payers for the doctor and two for the prescriptions. In a single-payer system, the doctor and the pharmacist get paid by one payer, not three and two, respectively. This occurs regardless of who employs the doctor and pharmacist, or what care the patient is receiving. Single-payer does not equal "socialized" or "nationalized" medicine. It simply means costs are paid by one source only, not two, three, or more sources. The best reason, however, to enact single-payer insurance through national public insurance is simple: risk spreading.

Risk spreading, risk pooling, and national public insurance

In any discussion of insurance, but especially in respect to health insurance, it is important to discuss the concepts of risk spreading and risk pooling. Simply put, risk pooling is literally "pooling" risks together. Suppose that you have a group of people, with some perfectly healthy and others chronically ill. If we put all of the healthy people together in one group and the sick people in another, we have begun pooling risk by identifying those who are the least risk (healthy) and those who are the most risk (sick). By doing this we, as an insurer, can charge different rates now to each group based on the different levels of risk exposure to us. The higher the risk (of actually having to pay a claim), the higher the premiums we charge that group.

Risk, in the most basic definition, is the chance that (in the case of an insurance company) the company might have to pay a claim. That is, the individual who has a higher chance of using the policy for medical care, in the case of health insurance, is a higher risk. So, if you have a chronic condition, such as diabetes, you will likely require more medical care, and therefore, are higher risk than someone with no medical issues. This explanation is, as I have said, very basic; it is not meant to be an academic definition. It is meant to provide a context for what we're talking about here. When we say risk what we really mean is the chance you'll actually use the policy, rather than just paying premiums for the policy without ever using it.

So, why do we pool risk? If you want to remain solvent as a company, you need to offset your losses with enough revenue. To limit your risk exposure, you need to offset higher risk by having more people who are considered lower risk as customers. The optimal solution would be to only have low risk customers and no high risk customers. However, low risk customers often don't need your insurance and thus many will opt out. So, a balance between high and low risk customers is sought, producing plenty of profit with as little risk as possible. To mitigate losses, the company excludes all individuals in groups whose risk is deemed unacceptable for your company. However, the inherent issue here is that those who need the care most are often the highest risk (since they will likely use the policy a great deal) and are therefore excluded.

As such, risk pooling produces "care rationing" and "death panels" (to use terms from recent memory). How do we get from risk pooling to death panels and rationing? It all comes back to that word – risk. As a means of limiting risk, insurers limit dollar amounts of care per year (and over a lifetime) - rationing - along with ever increasing deductibles and copays, shifting more of the cost onto policyholders and further reducing the risk to the insurance company. Have a condition that is covered, but a treatment that is not? In this case, the insurance company may refuse to pay for the treatment, or cancel your policy outright. Every insurer has a panel of doctors and bureaucrats who determine what treatments they will pay for and which they will not. These panels are, effectively, death panels. We all have our own stories of insurance not paying for this procedure or treatment when our doctor has told us it is what is needed. The decision to pay or not to pay come from these panels. Risk pooling does highlight groups of individuals who need special focus, but it should never be used as a tool of discrimination (which is how it has been utilized in this era of managed healthcare from our nation's oligarchy of insurance conglomerates).

Risk spreading operates differently than risk pooling. As the term suggests, risk spreading attempts to spread risk around, by increasing the size of the number of people in the pool rather than splitting people into even smaller groups. Let me use an example to better illustrate the differences. Suppose I decide to set up a lottery. In this lottery, everyone pays in $1 for a chance to win the jackpot prize of $100. To break even, I need at least 100 people to buy a ticket, if each person can only buy one ticket. Now, if any less than 100 buy tickets, I am bankrupt. Suppose instead that 1,000 people buy tickets and we increase the number of winners from one to five or 10. We still break even or turn a profit because five or 10 people winning $100 prizes with 1,000 people buy $1 tickets is breaking even or better. Now, let's suppose we increase the jackpot to ten $1,000 prizes and 20,000, 30,000, or 50,000 bought tickets. This is the power of risk spreading. By increase the size of the whole pool of participants, the risk of any one individual hitting that jackpot is reduced. Increase the number of participants enough and the risk is reduced, effectively, to zero.

Apply this to healthcare. Let's suppose you have 300 million Americans covered by one single-payer plan. Even if you have three million people who have serious medical needs at a given time, this is only one percent of the people covered, reducing the risk to almost zero. Three, six, nine, even 15 million at a time is, at most, five percent of those covered. Even the most expensive, most extreme medical care under such a large pool (spreading the risk) would amount to a negligible cost overall. Given that this single-payer plan would need to cover all Americans (natural-born and naturalized citizens), the best viable option is public insurance. It needs to cover everyone, and to do so, we all need to pay into it to fund it (via taxes).This represents lower costs than private insurance, and helps both citizens, businesses, and government.

A new single-payer system

When we say "universal healthcare" what we really should be saying is "single-payer healthcare," as we have already discussed. The question remains, though, as to what such a plan would look like, how would it be run, how much would it cost, and ultimately, would it be better than the current system. Let's address each of these questions, starting with what such a plan would look like.

To be a true single-payer plan, it would cover not just basic preventative care and major medical expenses (such as surgery), but would also fully cover mental health expenses, as well as diagnostic tests, specialists, and all other expenses associated with standard medical care (including emergency services). However, in an attempt to control costs, we would need to retain particular facets of current insurance, such as the primary care physician. Sure, you could seek a second opinion on a diagnosis, but not an eighth, ninth, or 15th opinion, as some do now. Furthermore, the plan would feature no co-pays or deductibles, as this would introduce a second payer, defeating the point of single-payer insurance. However, there is more yet to this plan, which is the inclusion of full vision and dental coverage as well (as we cannot simply ignore medical care for our teeth and eyes, as both are equally important to our physical and mental health).

There is one area I have not mentioned yet in the plan, and that is prescription coverage. Currently, prescriptions are absent (specifically, coverage for them) from many plans, or are included with fee schedules for different "levels" of drugs and various levels of co-pays, deductibles, and annual benefit caps applied for each of these different levels of drugs. Our societal drive to "live with" illnesses, rather than the pursuit of true cures and remedies has supported the bottom lines of large international pharmaceutical manufacturers and insurance companies. As the third component of our reformed single-payer system, we must include full prescription coverage as well. Americans should not be denied the prescriptions they need due to financial cost on their part, which is the point of having risk spreading and single-payer insurance in the first place.

Just to be clear, in place of Medicare, Medicaid, military, and private insurance, I advocate for a true, nationwide, single-payer health insurance program. This program would cover medical, dental, vision and prescription costs with no co-pays, no out-of-pocket expenses, and no deductibles.

Administration of the new single-payer system

There is a certain truth that private entities, rather than public ones, can attain a certain degree of efficiency and cost savings not present in the public sector due to the need to increase profits (primarily by reducing costs). However, there exists no reason to expect less, in terms of a focus on efficiency and cost savings, from publicly operated entities. One way we can achieve lower costs with better quality is a mix of public-and-private administration.

Single-payer health insurance is just that - insurance. It does not run hospitals, does not employ doctors or nurses (directly for the purposes of direct patient care), and does not operate pharmacies or employ pharmacists (again, directly for the purposes of patient care).

First, the nation would be divided regionally, allowing administration of smaller units rather than one large unit. The size of these regions will vary, but let's assume we divide the nation up into eight regions: northeast, southeast, upper central, mid central, lower central, southwest, central west, and northwest. Rather than create a whole new bureaucracy, staffed by federal employees, and entitled to federal retirement, we instead open bidding to existing insurance companies to operate as "agents" for the single-payer plan in the region they are bidding for.

There could be restrictions, included on how many regions a given company could bid to operate as agent for, that way we can encourage competition between these agents, and between regions, on various metrics such as cost savings from efficiency, quality of care, patient satisfaction, and overall health improvement through preventative care (such as reduction in number of individuals who smoke, or are overweight, as examples). The company selected (by winning the bid, and thus the contract) as regional plan administrators would then process all payment requests from all hospitals, care providers, and pharmacies, and would also be responsible for vetting each hospital, clinic, pharmacy, and staff listed requesting payment, to reduce fraud.

The agent cannot determine who is covered by the plan, but can, acting as agent for the government, refuse payment in cases of fraud, repeated requests for payment for the same procedure, or purely elective care. Care must be medically necessary and appropriate to be paid under the plan, and even though the decisions on care are made by doctor and patient, it becomes incumbent on the doctor to ensure medical appropriateness, rather than the desire to increase income, for procedures (if they wish to be paid under the plan). This does not mean insurance companies could not offer additional insurance to cover purely elective procedures. They could, but these companies, acting as agent, could not deny care just to increase their bottom lines if such care was deemed medically necessary, by the patient's primary care physician.

To ensure care anywhere, regardless of the agent handling local plan administration, all agents would need to pay claims by any American citizen presenting their national health card. This card would allow medical professionals anywhere in the country to access the patient's diagnostic history. Therefore, part of the plan would need to be the creation and maintenance of a national database, utilized by these agents, but also accessible by doctors, with authorization from the patient. Oversight of the contractual agents would come from the government through the creation of the United States Health Services Administration, or HSA. HSA would oversee contracting with agents, authorize payment on accounts, and operate the national health database. Operated in concert with the Department of Justice would be an HSA Office of Inspector General, pursuing fraud claims discovered by regional plan contractors and also investigating cases of denial of care. The job of the HSA is not to run hospitals or employ your local doctor, but to make sure all the components of the plan work together to ensure consistent, excellent, patient-focused care nationwide to all American citizens.

Costs of single-payer healthcare

According to an article from March 2009 by Fox News, many analysts predicted that the cost of single-payer universal health insurance over 10 years would be somewhere between 1.5 and 1.7 trillion dollars. Just to make it clear, that is $1,500,000,000,000 and $1,700,000,000,000. Often when people try and show the large numbers like that, they minimize that these are over ten years, not all at once. So, in reality, what they are saying is that the expected costs, at least in 2009 (and I doubt these have really changed much since then), were figured at around 150 billion to 170 billion per year. Given that we already bring in, as of 2010, 233 billion dollars in Medicare taxes alone, and single-payer insurance would allow elimination of Medicare and Medicaid (among other programs), single-payer insurance would actually SAVE money in the long run. Reports have shown this on a state-by-state basis since the early 1990s, and yet, during that time, we have had no movement on the federal level toward single-payer universal health insurance.

If we used taxes from the Medicare tax by itself, assuming that the revenue generated from that tax alone did not change (up or down) over 10 years, we could easily afford (costing NO additional money) single-payer insurance, nationwide, that costs up to 2.33 trillion dollars over 10 years without raising any new taxes, and without issuing any debt. This is something we can and should do. We can afford it; it puts control back in the hands of doctors and patients, not government or insurance bureaucrats, and ultimately ensures we have a strong, healthy population for the future - which benefits all of us.

Joshua R. Yates

Joshua R. Yates

Government Reform

To achieve real government reform, we must consider changes in how the government is structured, in terms of departments and agencies, the size of Congress and how we can streamline our government to improve its efficiency and make it more transparent, responsive, and accountable. We must remember that in our system, we ARE the government and the government is us. Therefore, if government is the problem, then we are the problem. I do not accept this; we are the solution, not the problem. We must be. We must look objectively at what is working, what is not, and what we want from our government. We all expect that our government will handle particular issues, such as national defense. We also expect that in times of national crisis or national emergency that the government will be able to do its role and restore order and provide some form of relief. Debatable is the government's role in environmental protection and of ensuring fair competition in the business world. Going further, it is also debatable if the government has any role in the economy as a whole, and if so, what that role is. There are many more questions worthy of serious discussion and civil debate that deserve answers. Questioning our government, what we want from it, and what its purpose is, is quintessential to our identity and history as Americans.

Why do we need government?

Government is, in the most general sense, the means by which we cooperate with one another to achieve mutual goals. Government is able to do specific tasks that benefit all of us, tasks that would be difficult or impossible for us to do individually. Construction of highways or bridges, operation and financing of fire brigades, city water and sewer networks, and providing law enforcement are all examples of the role of government. Thinking bigger though, government also has a particular role when it comes to providing national defense. Our nation was founded with a two-tier defensive structure. At its founding, both the militias of the states as well as the national army and navy were to be funded, trained, and provided for by government.

Government also provides what are called "public goods." Sure, we could each construct our own roads, have our own private armies for defense, and provide our own water and electricity, but what would ensure that the roads were constructed to uniform standards, or that the water was safe to drink? More than that, how could any one of us afford to purchase and maintain our own fighter aircraft, tanks, or other military arms individually for national defense? This is why these are usually done collectively by governments. Governments are able to pool the resources available to cover both the initial and ongoing financial costs as well as establishing uniform standards, which ensure that railroads link together properly, that bridges and roads are built uniformly, and that national defense and local public safety professionals are properly supplied and trained. Without government, the result would be, at best, piecemeal efforts at achieving any of these objectives. This was one of the issues of the Articles of Confederation and why the founders drafted a national constitution which created a stronger federal government. This does not mean that this experiment in a strong federal government has always worked well, or that there is not a place for state authority in our system. Far from it as the Tenth Amendment itself reserves to the states all powers not delegated in the Constitution to the federal government. Essentially, this is meant to say that any power not expressly delegated in the Constitution to the federal government remained the exclusive power of the states themselves. This was not and is not a free card for the states to usurp federal power; nor is it so narrow as to allow the federal government to deprive states of their rights either. It is a safeguard against either federal tyranny or a tyranny by the states, either individually or collectively. Without government, we are forced into a system where everyone is out for themselves, or mob rule.

A republic is, in the most basic sense, a government where the people (citizens) elect specific representatives to vote on their behalf in the government. This differs from a democracy in its purest definition. Simply put, democracy is the direct control of the government by the people, with every issue and every decision being put to a vote. The difference from a republic is more than stylistic. Do you and your neighbors elect someone who then votes for you all collectively as your representative or do you go to the polls yourself to vote on every issue, every time that the government needs to make a decision on anything? The difference is also apparent in what separates a republic from a democracy. Democracy is, truly, absolute tyranny of the majority. It is driven by opinion polls and trends, focused only on satisfying a base 51% majority, while both ignoring and indeed suppressing the opinion or will of the remaining 49%. Whatever way the 51% majority swings, so too does the democracy. Sudden, dramatic changes can occur in every election and on every issue. This does not provide stable or responsive government, it is little better than organized anarchy, and was a form of government that our founders were adamantly opposed to. A republic, by comparison, was intended to protect the minority from the majority by placing safeguards against the use of trends or polls as absolute guides to policy formation. Elected representatives would vote on behalf of whole groups of people, but not be absolutely consigned to vote according to the majority of their constituents if they felt it was in the best interests of all of the people. This smaller group of representatives was designed to minimize the influence and power of extremist factions, providing protection for the minority opinion against those of the majority. In practice, this has not always been the case. Our government has always been influenced by trends and emotions, including extremist factions, since its formation. It is part of the fabric of our American history. However, this does not mean that we should cast aside our republic in favor of a pure democracy, even though this is what some individuals have attempted to do over the past 100 years. We must resist the push for absolute democracy and fight to keep our nation a republic, lest we allow a total domination of our government (and ourselves) by a 51% majority, which is both easily manufactured and constantly shifting in its views.

Reforming to keep the Republic

In our fight to maintain a republic, we must remember what is the essence of a republic. What I mean by this is that we must accept that in a republic, we all agree that a smaller group making decisions on behalf of a larger group is a good thing. This power, however, must be protected to prevent it being controlled by any particular special interest. These representative leaders must speak for all of us, even if they do not speak for each of us individually. In other words, while I may not agree entirely with another individual on everything, as a representative, I would be expected to at least have a clear and complete understanding and appreciation for both my own viewpoint as well as of those in opposition to it – and to vote, as best I can, to best serve the interests of all of the individuals whom I represent. This does not mean that I, as representative, would always vote in favor of one view or the other. I must be flexible enough to vote the will of my constituents, even if I have opposing views personally. Ultimately, representing citizens is less about what I believe; it is about what the people that I represent believe. What I believe, my values and principles, certainly would be a facet in my decisions, guiding how I would represent the community which elected me, but I must also keep in mind that if I only represent those who agree with my own position I am doing a disservice to myself and all of my constituents. I will not always agree with the opposition, nor does it mean that I must always try and find some middle, third way on every issue. Our republic should not be a winner-take-all, absolutist approach to governance. It should not be one where a 51% majority dominates into submission the other 49%. If this were the case, our nation would be little better than one which is a pure, absolute democracy, where the majority dominates all and minority opinions are suppressed.

Our freedoms, guaranteed in our constitution (both the stated freedoms and the implied freedoms) are designed to protect minorities from persecution by majorities, and this is integral to our republic. Our Constitution prevents any one majority from having total control over every mechanism, every decision, every action of government, keeping large groups from subjugating small ones in our society. This is a good thing. It is what allows Americans to enjoy the greatest amount of freedom in the world. If we allow the desires of the majority to crush the desires of the minority, as some in recent years have argued for, we have a tyranny of the majority, which is, in reality, pure democracy, and is totally contrary to the republic that our nation was formed as.

In our goal to reform the republic, we must refrain from using labels, such as "liberal," "neoconservative," "socialism," or "socialist" (for example) against individuals, ideas, or government programs, and instead look to the structure of our government and the programs that we are funding, as well as how those programs are funded, for answers. Our reform must be meaningful, realizing real cost savings and streamlining our government so that we remove the weight of the heel of government, while maintaining the useful and necessary elements of our government.

Moving beyond labels

Commonly misused in our political discourse is the idea and label of "socialism." Socialism is not a political system, it is an economic idea. The idea that government has a more proactive role in society is not synonymous with socialism, but it is commonly mistaken for it. Socialism, by and large, involves the operation of businesses by the government, even if jointly with private owners, as well as the providing of vast services (i.e. public works, law enforcement, public education) by the government in the public interest. This may or may not involve wealth redistribution, and does not imply that the government controls the entirety of the economy, as is the case with command-style economies, commonly seen in Marxist-Leninist-Stalinist (often referred to as "Communist") states.

Another way in which the word "socialism" is inappropriately used is with respect to government regulation. For example, whenever an individual suggests that government should regulate a particular industry, or that we should protect social security or other social safety net programs, the charge of being a "socialist," or supporting socialism, is levied. The charge of being "socialist" as is being implied here is not new to American politics. Regulation is often called "socialist," even though the idea of regulation is itself not socialist. Government regulation can be present and beneficial in a capitalist society. Similarly, I hear comments from individuals charging that an unfettered market, supported by laissez-faire economic policies, is the true nature of the American economy, or rather, that it should be. These arguments are made that only if we have a completely deregulated "free market" economy can we truly adhere to the principles of freedom and democracy as supported by our founders. The issue here is that our Founders did not support a "democracy" but instead a "republic." While the two terms are used interchangeably, we should not confuse the two systems, and we should not allow economic policy to become somehow commingled with political systems in this respect. A country have a democratic system with a completely centrally-planned economy just as much as a country can have a "free market" economy with a totalitarian political system. To leave ad hominem attacks of being a "socialist" behind, we must recognize that our nation has embodied elements of "socialism" since its founding, and that is perfectly compatible with our political system. Being concerned with, and desiring regulation to prevent sludge from a nearby factory from being dumped into your local river, thereby polluting your drinking water does not make you a "socialist;" It makes you, instead, a concerned citizen. The facts that the government has both had the ability to regulate commerce, as well as contracts, are both forms of government regulation, and not all government regulation is bad. If you do not want to drink raw sewage, then you want government regulation. If you want to ensure that the food you are eating is not contaminated, then you want regulation. The list is not limited to these sorts of regulations, and they are extreme, but they do serve a point.

There are numerous examples of businesses within American history doing exactly these sorts of things in the pursuit of profit, and we must always assume that if there is a way to increase profit while making a cut elsewhere that businesses will move to increase their profit. Capitalism is not altruistic, and it never has been. It is not morally based. Capitalism, as an economic system, does not care about an equal distribution of wealth, nor is it concerned for the livelihood or welfare of any one, or group of individuals that are part of such an economic system. In the pursuit of profit, there is no stipulation in capitalism that business entities observe protections for their employees or their customers. Simply stating that customers could go elsewhere is not enough, just as telling employees to find other employment if they do not wish to work for low or no pay would also be inadequate. What is to prevent an employer from having you use equipment known to maim workers daily? Or to prevent them from serving diseased meat because they got it cheaper, and thus increased their profit margin? These are egregious examples, but only if we show the extremes can we understand the need for some regulations. That said, some regulations go overboard, and we should keep that in mind that the goal should not be total deregulation, but a balance between regulation in the public interest, in the interest of workers, and of businesses interest in sustained profitability. A balance must be sought, so the scales cannot be tipped too far in either direction.

Ultimately, labels such as "socialist" are inadequate, as we all want police, fire departments, and decent roads. We all want access to dependable electricity, at low cost, as well as clean, safe running water. All of these public programs are "socialism" as they are paid for by public monies to benefit all of us. They are what we call "public goods" and so we must examine not if we need these services, as we do, but how we pay for them to ensure that they are being funded appropriately and that we are not over or underfunding these services. We must also be open to the idea that there may, in fact, be other goods and services that are public goods and should be covered by government, such as, health care and broadband internet access. How these are handled, funded, and administered are all points for discussion. We must always remember that some regulation is good and that such regulation protects the public interest (the people), provided that we as citizens remain vigilant and ensure the balance between regulation and free enterprise is maintained, and never tilted too far in either direction.

Repairing the Republic

Our nation is in need of change, to fix what ails it. Americans are, and have always been, a divided people. Only once in our history did we ever have a truly one-party system, and that collapsed due to internal factionalism. Our divisions are what make us strong, even if we sometimes cannot see that at that exact moment. We are currently in the sesquicentennial (or 150th anniversary) of our Civil War, one of our most trying and divisive times in the history of our country. Our nation, quite literally, divided in two. We fought over ideas, beliefs, and desires for the future. In the end what we produced, even after years of civil war and over a century of subsequent growth, is a nation, which continues to remain divided in its ideas and opinions. Our political parties may change, ideological positions may shift, and views on particular issues may change, but what remains is that we, as a people, are dynamic and opinionated. Our willingness to express our opinions, even if others disagree, is part of what makes us Americans. It is what makes us resilient and what provides us the greatest opportunity to repair and renew our system for generations to come. Every generation in their own time must further changes and renew our political system again, for the situations they face, just as we do now.

So, how do we actually go about making real changes? We must look at three levels of government: national (or federal), state, and local. If we focus only on one of the three then we lose sight of the full scope of the needed reforms (and so I will cover each of the three separately). Bear in mind that my contemporary experience may differ from your own, and as you read this chapter (indeed, this entire book), you may have differing ideas or opinions, and that is great. This book is meant to provide insight for all of us to move forward on enacting real reform, not reform that changes nothing (or "illusionary" reform). That said, let's move together into the first set of needed reforms, at the national (or federal) level.

Federal Government Reform

The task of reforming the federal government could fill an entire book. One thing that we need to keep in mind as we are talking about reform, is that we cannot expect change to come entirely from within the system. In other words, we cannot simply expect that politicians, bureaucrats, or other insiders will change the system just because they say that they will. We, as the people, hold the power to change many things ourselves. We do this either by direct initiative (such as a popular ballot initiative, in many states) or most importantly by whom we elect to represent us in our government. Our vote is very important. We need to remember that our vote always counts, even if measures or candidates we support fail to pass or win election.

One point that merits discussion is the unfortunate reality that many of us do not vote, even though we have the right to do so. This can be due to a variety of reasons: polling stations in unusual locations, difficulty reaching the poll (due to schedule/time constraints, or other issues), or lack of knowledge about when the voting is open, difficulty registering to vote, and so forth. The number of issues is long, but ultimately, the issue is with barriers (either real or implied) preventing us from exercising our constitutional right to vote in our elections. So, many of us just do not participate at all. When we do, it is often minimal, relying on advertisements from politicians themselves or outside groups for cursory information on candidates or issues so that when we do vote, we vote as we are told. This might be seen as overly harsh in its assessment, or that I do not give enough credit to individual voters. I mean no disrespect to those who do vote, but we must acknowledge that many of us are so busy that we simply do not have the time to fully research issues or candidates presented to us on a ballot, and we therefore make decisions based on information we glean through media. This information is often minimal in terms of useful information, heavy on outright false or out-of-context information (misinformation), and is meant not to inform us, but to push us to vote "as we were told by the TV advertisement." Often, these commercials will feature half-truths or edited comments, video or sound clips meant to instill fear or blame, or completely manufactured information. This is, truly, engineered consent and manufactured politics.

Why do we allow this? Simple, because many of us do not vote, and those who do have not wielded the power of their vote in a way to say that they do not want misinformation politics to continue. How can we deal with this kind of intentional misinformation when both candidates and their surrogates are part of the problem? Denying them our money (in terms of donations) does not solve the issue, as the candidates or their Super PACs will simply turn to wealthy donors, corporations, or unions for funding. No, we must make it clear, through written letters or phone calls to all political candidates and officeholders that misinformation, intentional or otherwise, is unacceptable. If this does not work, I suggest placing candidates forward on the ballot who refuse to act in this fashion, make that known, and then run clean campaigns. Sure, some of these candidates might lose, but if we do it enough, we can make a difference, both conservatives and liberals. Vote whenever you have the option, make your opinion known, and step up through letters, telephone calls, or tweets to candidates and political parties that we want to vote, we demand our right to vote, and that we demand civility and real information for elections.

Expand the House of Representatives

Let's take a look at some specific reforms that we could realistically do to improve our government both in how it functions, but also in its responsiveness to us as citizens. In a republic, as mentioned earlier, citizens are represented in government by elected individuals, such as our House of Representatives. However, when many members of Congress, individually, each represent over 500,000 people it is impossible for these representatives to be able to even say that they truly represent the interests of even a fraction of their constituency. This allows fringe groups, such as lobbyists and special interest organizations, to exert a great deal of influence over these representatives, since it is possible that at least some sliver of the constituents in a given district will adhere to the special interest group's viewpoints.

The problem here is that this means that the representative no longer represents their citizen constituents, but instead represents some smaller special interest position, or some large donor (corporate, union, or otherwise) interest, rather than those of their citizen constituents who voted to elect them to office. Instead of directly communicating with citizens or being accountable to them, the representatives only need to worry about ensuring that their largest donors are happy so that they can pay for their campaign during election time and keep themselves in office. Staying in office then becomes the entire focus, rather than representing citizen's interests! This is not to say that there are not representatives that do their jobs diligently and honestly, but simply that there exists a very real question of who is really being represented by many members of Congress. This questions gives rise to ideas of having members of Congress wear the brands and logos of the groups whom they actually represent (the ones that fund their campaigns).

It seems that a major problem, then, is both money and influence in politics. While both money and influence are certainly a problem, they are simply a symptom and not the primary disease. The disease is that there are simply too few representatives, with districts (in many cases) that are just too big (some in terms of both geographic size, and in terms of population in the district). Limits to the number of representatives in the House is not contained within the Constitution, but instead has been limited by statute (public law). The statute in question is Public Law 62-5, or the Apportionment Act of 1911. This law limited the number of members in the House of Representatives at 435, and therefore is sometimes called the "435 Rule." Regardless of how many new states we would add, or how large the population of the United States might become, under this law, there would never be an increase in the number of seats in the House; only how they are distributed would change. The problem here is that this ensures that Representatives become more and more removed from their constituents, hidden behind PR teams, handlers, or other staff, insulating these representatives from the very people they are supposed to represent.

The solution to this problem is simple on the surface but offers very real benefits in the long run: increase the size of the House of Representatives by repealing Public Law 62-5. This would require, under the Constitution, for Congress to determine a new size of the house at each census, unless they simply create a mechanism that allows the number of representatives to grow based on the change in the census and then redistribute seats based on that new, (potentially) higher number. It would allow for changes in the size of the House based on real increases in population and real population shifts.

Couple this with the imposition of a cap on the number of individuals within a given district, which is to say that for each 30, 40 or 50,000 people (for example) the House must have a seat for a Representative. Granted, this does mean that the highest population areas (geographically) would exert greater control in the House, but ultimately the House is meant to be divided by population, so those regions with more people living within them would (and should) have greater representation. This prevents scenarios where a representative in South Dakota might have noticeably less constituents than the one from New York City, thus distorting (increasing in this case) the power of the less-populated area by diminishing that of the more heavily populated one. The House, compared to the Senate, is meant to be proportional based on population, and thus, we must be sure that everyone is being represented fairly, with adequate numbers of representatives in the House.

Other benefits of the larger House are twofold. First, it diminishes the power of money and lobbying in the political process. The sheer amount of money required to lobby the hundreds of new Representatives would be cost prohibitive. It is simply not feasible to afford to do this on a grand scale in every election, with every representative, nationwide.

Joshua R. Yates

Decentralizing the House of Representatives

Let's go even further than simply increasing the size of the House, let's decentralize it as well. We can do this by erecting (or acquiring) additional buildings in cities around the nation to serve as additional chambers of Congress. So, rather than Congress always convening in Washington, D.C., it would instead convene throughout the country, linked together in real time by video and audio teleconferencing software and cameras. This is where the second benefit comes in. By decentralizing the House, it brings the representatives closer to their home districts, and thus allows them to be in-district more often, and better serve their constituents. This also allows for a closer camaraderie between representatives through being closer to home (and thus more able to participate in functions with other members of Congress in their region), rather than pushing members of Congress to decide between camaraderie between colleagues or spending time in-district with their family and constituents. In terms of security and continuity of government in case of a terrorist attack, the decentralized Congress is a good idea. To attack one facility is easier than attacking multiple facilities simultaneously. Furthermore, having one facility destroyed, with the loss of its members, while horrifying, does not prevent the remainder of the body, placed throughout the country, from continuing to function. The House would have to appoint its own internal leadership in each region, with one primary Speaker (and Majority/Minority Leaders, of course) for the entire body, but who might be at any one of the particular regional chambers, depending on where they are elected from.

Having all of these additional representatives would certainly cost more money, right? Not to mention having to construct or buy these extra government buildings? Yes and no. Certainly the construction of new facilities will cost money; however, it offers us an opportunity to build facilities that will last for centuries, buildings that are testaments to our American society and culture, located throughout the nation, for all of us to be proud of. Furthermore, these costs are investments in our future, allowing for growth in each new facility by planning for that future growth today. The new construction also creates jobs, and in today's economic environment, these jobs will help propel our economy forward, along with real growth in our private sector from supplies and materials in support of this new construction. The cost in salaries and benefits for the new members can also be offset by the reduction in travel costs and additional costs as a whole from a reduction in the number of staff needed by each member. Staff who were eliminated initially would likely find themselves employed by these new members of Congress (due to the expansion in the number of representatives), thus allowing for a net reduction, overall, in staff expenses. So, we increase the number of representatives and reduce, per capita, the number of staff per member. This is good, and would keep costs down as we expand the size of the House of Representatives. Since members of Congress would also be closer to their home district, there is no reason for the individual representatives to have the large staff structure or PR machines that some currently have. This will allow greater opportunity for interactions between representatives and citizen constituents, and increase accountability to voters.

One question that I have been asked is how, exactly, does this larger House of Representatives benefit both citizens as well as other interests, such as business or labor? For citizens, it brings our representatives closer to home, allowing us the chance at greater access to our elected representatives in Congress, which is always a good thing. If we have greater contact with our representatives, they can do a better job at actually representing our interests in Congress. If we want to move beyond the era of constant polling and Congress being focused on reelection rather than representation, this is a vital first step. As for business and labor interests, the decentralized, larger House of Representatives also allows them easier access to the representatives closer to their place of business.

This is good because it ensures that while representing our interests, these representatives, being closer to home, can also see the real impact on businesses and meet with both business and labor leaders on a more frequent basis to ensure that legislation that is being discussed in Congress is taking into account their interests as well as ours. We elect representatives to act on our behalf, and to ensure that business and labor issues (both of which impact us as citizens) are being considered in legislation is a positive step. This does reduce the power of national lobbying organizations and collective groups (either business or labor), while strengthening the power of local and regional business organizations or labor unions.

The Executive Branch

Next, we need to take a serious look at the executive branch of our federal government and its various departments. The executive branch is much larger and more pervasive than when our nation was founded. This is both out of necessity as well as consequence of events throughout our nation's history. Our country certainly needs a strong executive branch, capable of performing all of the duties which we ask of it. However, we do not need an executive branch that is as pervasive in our lives as it is today. Our founders were concerned with an overly powerful executive, and that is, at this point in time, what we now have. Furthermore, redundancies between different executive branch agencies and departments produce inefficiencies that not only increase the financial cost of government, but also increase the level of government intrusion into our daily lives, perpetuating the ever-growing bureaucracy at the cost of liberty and freedom.

The main point I am making here is that we simply have too many agencies and too much power concentrated in the executive branch. Too often, multiple agencies perform strikingly similar tasks, which is the definition of redundancy. There are times where redundancies can be worthwhile; however, those cases are limited at best. Having three or four agencies (or their subagencies) whose tasks are nearly identical except those that are specialized in separate specific (yet closely related) areas produces the potential of jurisdictional overlap (or some other concern of whose job this really is). This redundancy (and waste) is entirely inappropriate for our government. We should be focused, to paraphrase President Calvin Coolidge, on making sure that our government is not wasteful (redundancy and inefficiency is waste) as waste by our government is denying income (as taxes and fees transfer income from citizens to the government) to people who need it, and who earned it. President Coolidge's comment, while paraphrased here, is as relevant to us today as it was in the 1920s when he said it. If we're going to have real, meaningful change at the executive level, we must start with a streamlining of executive agencies and departments.

Streamlining the Executive Branch

Our Constitution does not state that we should have, need to have, or must have the vast plethora of current departments and agencies that are part of the executive branch of our federal government. Sure, there are some departments and agencies of the executive branch that are constitutionally required, but the reach of the executive branch has expanded well beyond its initial constitutional mandate, particularly throughout the last century. The first step in reforming the extremely massive executive branch is to streamline its agencies and eliminate redundancies. This section is by no means comprehensive, but will highlight some cuts that can and should be made to begin the process.

One of the major roles of the executive branch is in law enforcement. While congress (the legislative branch) makes the laws, and the judicial branch interprets the law, it is up to the executive branch to execute, or enforce the law. However, that does not mean that we require multiple hyperspecialized agencies to facilitate effective federal law enforcement. In terms of law enforcement, just to name a few, we have the FBI (Federal Bureau of Investigations), the ATF (Bureau of Alcohol, Tobacco, and Firearms), the DEA (Drug Enforcement Agency), the USMS (United States Marshals Service), the USSS (United States Secret Service), and ICE (Immigration and Customs Enforcement) among many others.

While these agencies have different areas of specialization, and their separation might seem appropriate following Adam Smith regarding the division of labor (by specializing, we create efficiency in each task, rather than doing a lot of things only moderately well), the degree of overlap and redundancy in task (regardless of specialization) comes with a dollar cost. Each agency has its own support staff, its own buildings, its own protocols, and so forth, all of which cost additional money. If we want to reduce the cost of government, we must work to eliminate these redundancies, which means consolidation (or elimination) of agencies. Divisions between agencies with overlapping or similar tasks results, generally, in barriers to communication between agencies. In the past, rather than resolving these issues through agency consolidation, the response has been to create task forces (additional bureaucracies) or interagency committees to facilitate better communication and cooperation between these agencies. The hope has been that if we spend even more money, expanding the existing bureaucracy, that two people (or agencies) that weren't talking before might now talk because we added more people in the middle.

That is one of the most inefficient means of solving a problem that we have available, especially since it doesn't actually address the problem. It is equivalent to applying a small adhesive bandage to stop the bleeding after you just cut your arm off. You need emergency care and likely surgery, not an adhesive bandage from the grocery store. It's time for some surgery to fix this problem (not more bandages) and consolidation of these agencies is a good first step.

Some more concrete examples are the departments of homeland security, defense, and justice. First, none of these are expressly defined in the Constitution outright. Second, only two of these have historical precedent. Defense, previously called the Department of War and formed in 1789, has the longest historical precedent for its existence, followed by Justice, itself formed in 1870. The Department of Homeland Security, by contrast, was formed in 2002, and exists only as a bureaucracy over other bureaucracies. As I discussed earlier, this is the most inefficient solution to attempt to tie together multiple agencies.

One thing to remember is that all of these agencies, nearly every executive agency and department, are formed through acts of Congress, expanding or reorganizing existing bureaucracies. We can and should make cuts a part of consolidation while maintaining the ability of individual agencies, post-consolidation, to function efficiently. In every case, these remaining subagencies should be subject to performance audits to increase their efficiency and to eliminate further redundancies.

Reorganizing the Executive Branch

We will be covering a lot of shifting of agencies within the executive branch, but bear with me. I will provide a table at the end of this section to allow for quick review of the few agencies I propose we move at this time, where they should move to, and those agencies that should be eliminated entirely. Remember, this is not a complete comprehensive list of all agency reforms that are needed, but some that should be dealt with first. I will also periodically use some of the acronym names for agencies, such as DoJ for Department of Justice. It should be shocking to all of us just how many agencies we have that comprise the bureaucratic apparatus of the executive branch, but we can cut through it and in the end create a leaner, more efficient, and fully functional executive branch to move us forward in this century.

Department of Homeland Security

The Department of Homeland Security must be abolished. Aside from the historical analogues found in fascism, communism, and dictatorships with their own secret police forces or internal security forces, the entire idea of such a bureau or department as part of our government contradicts with the idea of individual liberty that our nation was founded on. If we are to be watched every moment, of every day, in the interests of total national security, then we are no longer free, but a slave to our government and its will and desires. Rather than a government of the people, by the people, and for the people, we would have a people of the government, for the government, and by the government and its decrees. There is no guarantee of absolute security in our Constitution, only a guarantee of life, liberty, and the pursuit of happiness. So, by our own national ideal, the idea of "homeland security" or even "national security" is anathema. Let us not forget that our very founders could easily have been called terrorists by the British at the time, yet we look to them as patriots and visionaries. They fought so that we could be free of a state where the pursuit of security trumped individual liberty. We should always remember that and stand firm against any attempt, as those that have occurred in the past decade, to erode our liberty in the name of security.

The pursuit of "homeland" security is expensive, and is intrusive. Go to an airport today, and you will be subjected to groping by a minimum-wage "security official" from a subagency of the Department of Homeland Security, known as the Transportation Security Administration. At the same time, you may be subjected to x-ray scans, or other invasive measures that we are told are meant to protect us.

However, the problem here is that this "security theater" does not produce any security, but instead is an overt erosion of personal liberty and was exactly what terrorists sought when they attacked our nation on September 11, 2001. In a truly free society, the easiest victory for a terrorist is to instill fear through terror. This fear causes a restriction on freedom and liberty and produces police states, nations obsessed with national security above all else. Thus, the terrorists win. To actually counter a terrorist and prevent their victory, you have one option: not to be afraid or succumb to fear and terror. By creating these intrusive agencies that are meant to "protect us" by subjecting us to violations of our freedom and liberty, we have handed victory to terrorists. Victory for a terrorist is not in the deaths that they cause, but in the fear, terror, and societal change they are able to enact as a result. Therefore, terrorists don't actually have to attack us again, as they now know that the mere thought that they might attack us is enough to cause further erosion of freedom and liberty, and they know that we will accept the loss of what makes us American without question. This servile

I am reminded of the phrase from my Catholic upbringing, in particular Psalm 23:4 ("Yea, though I walk through the valley of the shadow of death, I will fear no evil: for thou art with me; thy rod and thy staff they comfort me."). How can I say that we should not be afraid when terrorists kill thousands of people in our country or around the world? I say it because I am resolute in my faith in God that regardless of what any terrorist might do to me or any of us that He went before me into death, and that by His action I have nothing to fear because He will always walk beside me. When many of us were horrified, rightly so, and terrified on September 11, 2001, I was reminded of the words of Pope John Paul II in his book Crossing the Threshold of Hope *where he reminded all of us that we should remain strong, remembering Jesus' own words to his disciples to "Be Not Afraid." As terrible and horrifying as September 11th was, no actions of any terrorist can ever measure up to or even remotely rival the awesome power of God. Thus, while I was as angered as any of us on that day, I felt that we as a people should not sacrifice who we are or what makes us American (our freedom and liberty) out of fear produced by the actions of a group of terrorists. I have faith in God, and refuse to surrender liberty and freedom because a small group of individuals, using terror and death, want me to do so. I am an American, and I love my God, my freedom, and my individual liberty too much to willingly give it up in the name of (supposed) security.*

fear should be opposed by all Americans, especially those of us who are Christians, as it runs counter to our religious faith.

I personally dislike the idea and existence of the Department of Homeland Security, as I have made abundantly clear, and feel that it is simply the creation of a bureaucracy for the sake of directing other bureaucracies, which is inefficient. The question remains, however, what do we do with all of the different agencies that were placed under the umbrella of Homeland Security? The solution is to move these agencies into the departments that are most in-line with their stated mission and objectives. Only one agency of Homeland Security would be completely eliminated in this proposal, that being the Transportation Security Administration. Given my disdain at the trading of liberty for "security theater," the TSA is the overt manifestation of that disdain. There already exist other agencies which better understand how to examine populations for potential risks rather than subjecting a free people to an invasive security theater regime.

Aside from the TSA, however, we still several other agencies to move. First, the Coast Guard (our nation's true fifth branch of military service) moves to the Department of Defense (DoD), along with the Border Patrol. Protecting our coastal and inland waterways and seaways is protecting our borders. The two belong with Defense, and should be held to the same standard of training, and receive the same level of funding, scrutiny, and investment as our other land, sea, and air military forces. This will allow a level of coordination between these two national defense forces and our other armed forces to protect us against real threats in a more expedient, cost effective, and efficient manner.

The United States Secret Service does more than simply protect Presidents (current and former), Vice Presidents, and such. They also are active, as an example, in counterfeiting and major fraud investigations. In the past, prior to the creation of Homeland Security, the Secret Service was part of the Department of the Treasury. However, while they do deal with currency, securities, and fraud, their other duties make them more suited to placement within the Department of Justice (DoJ), and this is where I would move the agency. This will allow better coordination of their activities with other federal law enforcement agencies, all of which should be under the umbrella of DoJ, rather than mixed throughout the various departments of the executive branch.

Prior to the creation of Homeland Security, immigration enforcement and customs enforcement existed as separate agencies (U.S. Immigration and Naturalization Service and U.S. Customs Service, respectively), and should be split again into two agencies. Their functions, while both dealing with borders and either people crossing our borders (immigration) or goods that are crossing the borders (customs), they are not similar and should not be housed under the same agency. Immigration Enforcement will return to its prior name, the U.S. Immigration and Naturalization Service, and be placed within the Department of State. Customs Enforcement will likewise return to its prior name, as the U.S. Customs Service, and be placed within the Department of the Treasury. Immigration and Customs Enforcement (ICE), as it exists today, would be eliminated.

Along with the movement of the reinstated Immigration and Naturalization Service to the Department of State, Citizenship and Immigration Services will be placed into the Department of State and merged into the Immigration and Naturalization Service (INS). There is no reason for the two to be separate subagencies, with separate facilities, staff, etc. The cost of separation does not make fiscal sense. There is no reason that INS could not simply have a subdivision which focuses on enforcement activities. We need these two to operate together, so that we can realize gains from their integration both in speed, efficiency and cost. By placing the two together, we can reduce costs from redundancy that might otherwise have remained in the system, either through the cost of additional, redundant staff, or additional unnecessary facilities.

Another agency we need to address is the National Protection and Programs Directorate. This is another example of a bureaucracy created to oversee other bureaucracies. In essence, the government has created a bureaucratic middleman between the Department of Homeland Security and four agencies it is supposed to oversee. So we have three levels of bureaucracy to deal with now. Another oddity, the Federal Protective Service, which operates security services for federal buildings, is placed here instead of being placed in a department where it can best integrate with other agencies, such as in the Department of Justice or perhaps the Department of State. Given that we are moving the Secret Service to the Department of Justice, we should do the same with the Federal Protective Service. The remaining components of this directorate should be shifted under the oversight of the Director of National Intelligence. These offices are all focused on risk prevention and on protecting national assets from attacks, internal or external. Coordination of this information and these offices with the intelligence community directly would provide a great deal of benefit. Put them where they belong, under the Director of National Intelligence, and then abolish the National Protection and Programs Directorate.

Lastly, the final major agency of Homeland Security that we need to address is the Federal Emergency Management Agency, or FEMA. FEMA has a bad reputation after their mishandling of the aftermath of Hurricane Katrina. They do serve a useful purpose, however, in allowing the federal government to marshal resources to specific locations in the event of a serious event, such as a natural disaster. However, they need to not be an agency of national security, but an agency focused on relieving strain and trauma during major disasters. They are not an agency of national defense, nor do they perform any sort of law enforcement. Instead, they move resources where they are needed and coordinate efforts in the aftermath of an event. As such, since they are entirely support focused, and should rightly be, I suggest moving FEMA to the Department of the Interior. That department already has a variety of tasks that it addresses; there is no reason that it should not also address natural disasters as well.

Department of Health

Currently, this department is called the Department of Health and Human Services. The reorganization of this department drops the phrase "human services" as the focus should be on health. Human services, as a term, is redundant unless this department somehow excludes non-human services, and thus is dropped from the name. As the Department of Health, this now reorganized department will perform some of the same duties it does now, with respect to its various sub-agencies. We can look at those agencies, however, and find cost savings. With the dissolution of Medicare and Medicaid, as I discuss in the chapter on entitlement reform, and its replacement with a universal single-payer health insurance system, we no longer have need for the Centers for Medicare and Medicaid Services, or CMS.

What we do need is an administration that serves as the chief administrating agency for the single-payer system. I have tentatively called this agency the United States Health Services Administration, or the HSA. The HSA would both coordinate the regional agent contracting process (allowing for regional agents to serve as agents of the government and administer the health program in a more efficient manner than a government bureaucracy) and also provide payment on medical claims processed by the regional agents. Furthermore, the HSA would provide oversight of the regional agents, ensuring quality, cost, and performance criterion are being met. In addition, HSA would oversee the creation, maintenance and operation of a new national health database, which would allow regional agents and health service providers access to relevant medical information, so that any U.S. citizen who presents their health card can receive care at any health facility in the United States.

Going one step further, while I do advocate for a national, universal single-payer system (which Medicare in its current setup is not), the federal government needs to get out of the business of operating hospitals. There is a vast difference between a single-payer health insurance plan and a socialized health care system that controls both the insurance AND the health facilities (including employment of physicians). In this case, while I feel that the best solution is a single-payer health insurance, administered by private contractors but controlled (ultimately) by the taxpayers through the government, we do not and cannot have government control of health facilities or physicians. The HSA will oversee the sale of government controlled hospitals to private industry. Private industry can allocate the capital resources more effectively than the government. All that the government does, in this system, is ensure payment on claims presented by physicians through the contracted agents (serving as regional administrators on behalf of the HSA). Decisions on care are made exclusively by the patient and their physician, with oversight against fraud and excessive or wholly unnecessary care (to reduce costs) by the contracted agents, who are then overseen by this HSA. Don't confuse this with a health maintenance organization (HMO) – there are no networks, you choose your physician; you and your physician determine, together, treatments plans for your situation (not a bureaucrat). There is no bureaucratic middleman deciding your care. There are no death panels. These contracted agents aren't picking your care for you, or usurping power from you and your doctor. They are simply, but effectively, watching for fraud within the system.

Medical personnel currently in the employ of the federal government would be transferred to the HSA. In time, as control of facilities shifts to private control, some of these employees can likely be shifted to private industry as well. However, this may take time, and at the minimum, a freeze on new federal hiring at these facilities should be implemented thus allowing for the elimination of positions through attrition over time (via retirements or departures from federal service). The only personnel that I do not foresee moving to private industry outright are military medical personnel, serving both in the field and in military-operated hospital facilities. That is, in this case, the one exception to the private employment objective for all medical personnel in the United States.

Federal Housing Administration

Currently, the Federal Housing Administration (or FHA) is an agency of the Department of Housing and Urban Development. As we renamed the Department of Health and Human Services to the Department of Health, we shall also rename the Department of Housing and Urban Development to the Federal Housing Administration and limit the scope of its activities to those currently handled by the existing FHA: housing. However, I intend to go further than simply renaming the department. Due to changes in the Department of Commerce (which we will discuss shortly), this now renamed agency will cease performing any of its "urban development" functions: such as community development block grant programs, loan guarantees, economic development grants, empowerment zone grants, and disaster recovery grants. Urban development is economic growth, and these functions will be taken care of with changes to the Department of Commerce. Housing, specifically the policy initiatives to encourage individual homeownership will be the purveyance of the new FHA. We can examine its specific policies later, if desired, but at this point, it is easier to work with the agency as a whole. Additionally, FHA shall be reduced from a cabinet-level agency to an agency under the Department of the Interior. The Director of this agency will report to the Secretary of the Department of the Interior, rather than directly to the President.

Why not simply remove the agency? There is still a purpose for having the federal government, in conjunction with local and state government, encourage individual homeownership in the United States. Assisting in securing of mortgage loans for home-buyers, ensuring that discrimination is not occurring in mortgage banking as well as prohibiting discrimination with rental proper-ties is a worthwhile task for the agency. That said, the federal gov-ernment needs to get out of the business of actually operating (and subsidizing) properties. In many cities the "housing projects" have ended, and been demolished. In other locations, however, they con-tinue. Rather than encouraging individuals to work to break the chains of poverty, these housing programs harm individual growth and development, punishing instead of encouraging individu-als to break out of poverty. It is another holdover from the chains placed on vast segments of society out of the social engineering of the "Great Society" initiatives of the 1960s. Given the opportunity, Americans have always shown resiliency and perseverance, over-coming supposedly insurmountable odds to achieve great success.

Homeownership is one of these elements of the "American Dream" that has been denied to too many through government housing projects or subsidized housing. Further, the goal of home-ownership has been again denied to many as a result of banks issuing mortgages to those who were not financially ready. Those without financial means to afford their homes were induced to buy with offers of no upfront costs, no money down, 125% mortgages, or were offered other "subprime" options. This allowed banks and builders to acquire short-term profits, and in the process hurt everyone. After the collapse, they played fast and loose with the law, foreclosing on individuals without the due diligence needed to ensure the foreclosure was legitimate in the first place. In both of these cases, a stronger, better-focused FHA could have served as a check to ensure that homeownership was the goal, and that both individuals, banks, and builders are doing each other justice and pursuing the goal of the "American Dream" of one's own home fairly and without shortsighted concepts such as zero-down loans or robo-signed foreclosures.

In our pursuit of an FHA that encourages homeownership we must make a few changes to existing laws to support this. First, we must amend the U.S. Housing Act of 1937, in particular Section 8. Income-controlled housing (which caps the amount of income tenants can earn annually), allows the landlord to assess rent to the tenant but also assess the difference between what the tenant is paying and what the landlord desires to be paid by the government. Landlords will construct entirely new apartment complexes, or whole new subdivisions of single-family homes, and then turn them into income-restricted rentals under Section 8. Additional needed changes (and these are again not comprehensive but meant to be a good start) are the termination of the Housing Choice Voucher Program. This program supports the creation of housing to keep families impoverished by insisting they remain at or near the poverty line or face eviction. The rent, which is still not cheap for the tenant given the severe income restrictions, therefore amounts to a gouging of the tenant and the government by opportunistic landlords.

The concentration of poverty-stricken individuals into small communities then continues to perpetuate the culture of poverty. By ending this program, we are essentially ending government rental subsidization in the United States. This is simply step one in the larger solution. Next, we must also eliminate the programs which subsidize poverty further, such as the Section 8 Moderate Rehabilitation Single Room Occupancy (SRO) program. This program, similar to the one I just discussed, provides for monies to "rehabilitate" buildings for use as housing for impoverished individuals with extremely low incomes. Not only does the program pay for the renovations, it also pays future owner costs for owning and maintaining the property.

With all of this money being paid out, how are these still privately owned? For all intents and purposes, this property is now owned by the government. This is just as insidious as the previously mentioned Section 8 program, and encourages a culture of poverty and acts as an inducement for businesses to remain in the game of continuing the culture of poverty. The objective at hand is to END the cycle of poverty and bring people out of poverty. Programs such as these do not serve that end and must be abolished.

Instead, we should consider reexamining the currently defunct program called "HOPE for Homeownership of Single Family Homes," known as HOPE III (or HOPE 3). This program was originally designed to provide funds to lower-income Americans with the purpose of purchasing or renovating a home they wish to buy. With the vast number of foreclosures, and a current shift (which is disconcerting) to a renter society, the reorganized FHA should be tasked with restarting programs focused on providing either down payment assistance or renovation assistance for those Americans who qualify for a mortgage loan to encourage them to move from renting to homeownership. There was once a drive in this country for everyone to own their own home, and we should have that same push again. However, we must be certain that we are encouraging responsible homeownership.

A program that has not been funded in over a decade is the Section 8 Welfare to Work program. Given the changes in public assistance that I discuss in the chapter on entitlement reform, a housing initiative that assists individuals in securing permanent homes, that they own, is a positive means to encourage both job stability and further growth. Reinstating this program will also show, through success of participants, that poverty can be overcome and will instill in children the truth that they can achieve the "American Dream" themselves with hard work and perseverance. This program should be integrated in the mandate of the new FHA to encourage homeownership in the United States for everyone. Since we are already pushing individuals to work as a means of providing assistance through the new WPA-style program I discussed, so too can we support the goal of homeownership for those currently renting. Those currently in the new WPA program should also have a means of working toward homeownership as well. You work, get paid, learn a skill (either skills training or retraining), and the government sets aside a stipend (separate from your pay) toward down payment on a home of your own. This can be coupled with other programs encouraging homeownership (outside of those currently seeking aid through the new WPA) but is an additional way through which we can break the cycle of poverty, encourage homeownership, and get America moving forward again by renewing the reality of the American Dream. This stipend would continue accruing even after one had moved to regular employment (after the WPA program), and therefore, help continue encouraging homeownership over time.

The final component of change within the FHA is the funding of educational grants for students, with mandatory years of employment with the FHA upon graduation. As a graduate student, research grants are a vital component to completion of graduate study. In particular, those students currently pursuing their Ph.D. degree commonly seek research assistance in the form of grants. Some Master's degree candidates do as well. There were once a series of programs operated by HUD which provided grant monies to students pursuing their doctoral (Ph.D.) degree, to support research which was related to the mission of HUD. Other government departments, such as the Department of State and the Department of Agriculture, still do this. In exchange for a number of years of funding, the student agrees to work as an intern for the department when not actively studying (essentially the summer break) and agrees to work for the department after they graduate for each year paid for by the government. This benefit ensures the government has well-educated individuals to administer programs and oversee policy development. This keeps the government efficient, and helps to ensure that new sets of eyes are always looking at these programs, which works to counter the trend by government to stagnate and maintain the status quo.

Department of Commerce

Another department which should undergo changes is the Department of Commerce. For the most part, I have kept much of the department as it is currently organized. First, however, we should move the National Oceanic and Atmospheric Administration (NOAA) out of Commerce and into the Department of the Interior. As the U.S. Geological Survey is already a part of the Department of the Interior, there is no reason why NOAA should not also be part of the same department. However, the real changes that we need to make to the Department of Commerce involve the creation of a new undersecretary position (Undersecretary for Development and Growth), and a new agency, the Business Development Administration.

Into the Business Development Administration I have consolidated the Small Business Administration as a sub-agency, its director becoming an assistant secretary. In addition, I have created a new sub-agency called the Joint Development Administration (JDA), led also by an assistant secretary. The Small Business Administration would remain focused largely as it is today, with some internal streamlining and programs being reviewed for effectiveness and modified as needed. The Joint Development Administration would be tasked with overseeing a new initiative to help grow new businesses, not simply small business (which is the focus of the SBA). The JDA would oversee new public/private partnerships and investments made on behalf of the government in private industries. Rather than subsidies or tax breaks as a means of encouraging internal business growth and development, the federal government can pursue policies through the Business Development Administration that encourage repatriation of capital assets by existing businesses as well as growth in new businesses that will create jobs here, employing both the present and next generations of Americans. The Economic Development Administration, the Minority Business Development Agency, and the National Telecommunications and Information Administration would be moved under the Business Development Administration as well. To be consistent with other agencies of the BDA, the national director of the Minority Business Development Agency will instead be titled as assistant secretary for minority business development.

I have stated my frustration at the idea of creating bureaucracies to oversee other bureaucracies. In this case, I want to be clear that the Business Development Administration is not intended to be an overseer of other bureaucracies. Instead, it is intended to be an integrated approach to government support for the development of private industry, to the point of entering into joint partnerships within certain fledgling new industries. States are already testing this approach; the federal government should as well.

State Government Reform

Unfortunately, many of us in the United States do not pay much attention to our state governments. We often focus only on national politics and government. If we do discuss state politics, it is often only gubernatorial politics. However, our nation is meant to be a patchwork of individual states, each with its own laws, ideas, and views on how things should be done. A classic example of this is in how our federal Constitution is amended. Congress might pass an amendment, but unless it is ratified by the states, the amendment does not become part of the Constitution. In this way, we have codified the power of our states to control our federal government.

The very idea that a state can nullify federal laws or provisions on its own is contrary to the nature of our union. Don't take this to mean that I support secession or other extreme states' rights provisions. Nullification (in other words, states can nullify federal law) was ruled out in the mid-19th century. However, states can exercise a great deal of power within their own borders as well as how they function as part of our nation. Sure, they cannot impose restrictions on elected officials at the federal level (such as term limits), but they CAN impose limits on their own legislators and statewide officials. Many states already do. The main point here is that it is an unfortunate reality that many of us cannot name all of our state officials nor our own state legislators. We are often familiar with issues of debate on the national level (which, granted, is the main focus of this entire book). However, we cannot and must not forget to address those issues which are relevant in our own states, and recognize the need to resolve those issues, not just those at the federal level.

While the federal government can impose laws which affect us all, the laws passed in our statehouses are closer to home and can impact us just as much. Real change must be achieved in our own states, starting with a demand for accountability and efficiency from, and within, our own state governments.

Why demand efficiency from our states? If our states, which are smaller in size and scope than the nation as a whole, cannot achieve some degree of efficiency and remain accountable directly to their citizens, then how can we expect the much larger and more unwieldy federal government to do so? Many of the ideas and objectives discussed in this book can easily be applied to state governments, and even local government. A prime example of these objectives is tax reform.

As discussed in the chapter on tax reform, one of the plans that I agree with is the FairTax. The plan for a consumption tax, rather than income taxes, can easily be applied to any state. Nearly every state collects both income and sales taxes. The apparatus already exists for a shift to a consumption tax, and the abolition of income tax levied by states. There is a specific need for efficiency from our state governments, to whom we pay taxes, elect legislators and other officials, and to whose laws and constitutions we are also bound beyond those of the federal government.

We must be vigilant at our state level, just as at the federal level, and we must do everything in our power (as citizens) to vote in our state elections and become knowledgeable about our state government, and those who seek to serve us as state officials. We must demand that our state governments justify their tax revenue, where it is being spent, how much is being wasted, what is being done about it, and then we must hold them accountable for it. Government exists, at all levels, to serve us, not the other way around. Take a stand, make it count, and create an impact by holding state government accountable. We absolutely must spend as much time and energy in vetting and electing quality state legislators as we should with federal candidates. Our republic requires strong, competent state governments.

Local Government Reform

The final element to government reform is often ignored: local government. Often, in discussions about government reform, it is almost universally about the national government. State government is generally discussed as a side note. Even though I mention state government in this book, it is mainly to address federal issues. Many of the same concepts and ideas, however, could easily be applied to state government. Local government has the potential for the greatest noticeable impact in our daily lives. Local ordinances can cover issues such as where you can drive, where you can walk, what you can do, where you can do it, when you can do it, and so forth. Our daily lives are often under the control of our local governments and it sadly tends to receive the least attention from voters. Too many examples abound, of communities like Oak Grove, Missouri, a community whose roads are left crumbling while its aldermen argue about the sand content under a proposed statue. These aldermen also complain that their constituents don't vote, but make no attempt to engage their constituents or encourage voting in local elections. Almost all of us have an opinion on national politics. Fewer openly appear to have an opinion on state politics, or know who their state officials are or what they specifically are supposed to do. Even fewer will know who their local city or county/parish officials are, what they do, or what the different tax rates are (for example) in their community. How many of us can say, with certainty, what our local sales tax rates, school tax rates, or property tax rates are? Who are all of the members of our local school board, city council, or county commission? When is the next meeting of any of these government bodies? How many of these officials are appointed, rather than elected? How much do they get paid and where does that money come from? These are the questions we should be asking, yet too few of us do.

Local government is not exempt from the demand for accountability and efficiency. In many cases, the elected city council appoints (hires) an unelected city manager or administrator to control the city government. Some counties do this as well. If we are concerned with liberty and freedom, we cannot forget local government, as they have the greatest opportunity to rob us of our liberty and our freedom through ordinance and regulation.

I mentioned the city manager and administrator, noting that in places those are employed that they are often appointed, not elected. My personally belief is that such arrangements shift the power from the people to bureaucrats. While the city manager may be accountable to the city council, and the councilors are accountable to the people, this adds an extra layer of bureaucracy and strips control over the government from the people and gives it to the government itself. Instead of being able to vent our dislike of our local government and its policies by voting out council members who supported policies that we opposed, we are left with the city manager, who is not elected, who can (theoretically) continue in their job even if we change a few council members. This places the power to change the government not with us, but with the council members that we elected, hoping that they will take action and remove the city manager. Sure, the city manager may work at the pleasure of the city council, who works for the people, but this is not enough. There is no direct recourse for citizens to remove the city manager. Local government is the closest to us, and should be the most responsive. That means ensuring that we, as the citizens, can vote out officials we disapprove of (based on policies they supported or helped to enact), rather than replacing some officials but being wholly unable to replace others. Power must reside in the hands of the people, not unelected bureaucrats who are themselves shielded from responding to the will of the people through the vote.\

We, as voters, must expect more from our governments. Government, especially local government, must show its sources of revenue, and we must hold them accountable to why they require that revenue, what they are doing with it, and what the purpose of those programs are.

Subsidy Reform and Business Development

One way in which our government facilitates economic growth is in the form of a subsidy. A subsidy is the transfer of money from the government to a private enterprise for any number of reasons. Also keep in mind that not all subsidies involve the government transferring actual money from itself to a business. Tax breaks are a subsidy as well. In exchange for allowing a business to retain more of its revenue (rather than pay that money to the government in taxes) the tax break essentially leaves the money within the business itself, allowing the business to utilize it as it sees fit in the pursuit of mutual goals between the business and the locality offering the tax break. This could result in additional employees being hired, new capital construction, or other benefits for both the business and the locality. This is not always a bad thing. Rather than collect the money, which involves layers of bureaucracy and cost on the part of the government, the tax break subsidy is more efficient. What we need to investigate is not eliminating all government subsidies (as they do serve a needed purpose in economic growth) but determining which subsidies to retain, at what level of subsidization, and to determine if particular subsidies are still necessary at this point in time.

No government support should be eternal. The purpose of a subsidy should be to encourage growth and development of business, but not have business reliant or expecting government aid and support. Generally speaking, subsidy support should encourage investment in particular industries (i.e. agriculture, oil and gas exploration, and so on), or growth of new industry to keep American businesses at the forefront of business growth and development globally. This subsidy reform is intended to change the relationship between the government and business, removing the government from much of the equation outside of a few key purposes.

First (mentioned previously), I proposed the creation of a Joint Development Administration, tasked with administering a new set of programs designed to turn government support into a results-driven model, with the government providing additional venture capital in key industries, such as developing better electric motors and batteries for our vehicles. This style of government investment has been done before in our own past, as well as within other nations, such as Japan during the Meiji, where Japan experienced rapid industrial and economic growth. In the case of the Joint Development Administration, the U.S. Government (rather than providing a subsidy in the form of cash payments or tax breaks) would provide investment funds, holding a portion of the company stock (similar to an investor in early rounds of initial funding), and retain board membership in any company that is being developed jointly through the JDA.

This does not preclude outside investment, instead it allows for the government to act as an investor, alongside private capital. With the government serving as an additional investor in these new businesses, it allows faster, more robust growth in industries that will be vital to our future as a country. As these are results-driven investments, the government would be looking to eventually "cash out" of these businesses, selling their stake once the business is stable. This might be during, or after, an IPO or perhaps during a later round of financing. Furthermore, the government might be an investor in only one round of financing, but the program would not be limited strictly to one round only. Companies that show promise might warrant additional investment, a decision that would need to be made on an as-needed, individual basis. This program does not, and must not, require continual investment if the company is able to find other financing.

Additionally, the JDA would serve as a means to connect new businesses with potential outside, private investors, joining forces with private capital to invest together in new ventures. These additional investments should generate positive revenue for the program, and thus for the government, while creating new jobs and empowering new businesses in America, while promoting entrepreneurship and maintaining private ownership of American businesses. As the driving goal for the JDA is to eventually exit any businesses which it is invested in, this arrangement is not designed, or intended, to produce government-controlled businesses. This is not socialism, it is designed solely to provide responsible government assistance in the spirit of free enterprise and capitalism. It is a positive relationship between business and government in a way that promotes independent business growth and development without permanent subsidies.

Most likely, though, there still exists an inevitable question about the degree of government involvement in these businesses, and what the relationship would be between the businesses and the government. The question of what happens should other private investors pull out of the company still remains. In such a situation, the government would likely be the remaining investor, appearing as that the company was entirely government owned. The fact that government is the final investor does not make the business a failure. Instead, the government and the company management would need to look at the means to either draw new investment in the company (by selling off portions of the government's share), or liquidate the assets of the company (such as in bankruptcy), allowing the government to recoup some of investment (at the least, mitigate its losses). There may be cases such as this where these businesses fail, causing the government to take a loss on its investment. However, these losses can and should be offset by gains made from successful businesses funded through the JDA. As with any form of investment (or even subsidy), there is a potential for a loss. Properly managed, however, the JDA should produce a net gain for the government, producing a net profit, which can then be utilized by the government to make new investments, fund existing obligations or retire outstanding federal debt, as examples. The staff and administrators of the JDA should be experienced with business reorganizations, investments, and familiar with the intricacies of venture capital. If this means bringing in venture capitalists to help administer the JDA, then so be it. The JDA would work closely with venture capitalists, and having individuals who have been part of the venture capital business industry working closely with (or for) the JDA will be vital to its success.

The Small Business Administration, or SBA, would serve as another means of government assistance to businesses, much as it does now by focusing on small businesses, and providing loans (rather than direct investment). The SBA should focus on true small businesses, including home businesses or small family businesses. It should also be providing better, more frequent, and more readily available access to counseling and support on business issues as needed by our small business owners. It should provide access to support services that businesses need, whether it be outside payroll support services and benefits administration or some other business expense essential to operating a small business. The goal is for small businesses to remain an engine for economic growth in our nation (as they are today) and to encourage individuals to step into business ownership themselves, if they so desire. Entrepreneurship has been a driving force in our economic growth throughout our entire history. It should continue to drive growth in the future, and a solid SBA, to compliment the new JDA, is critical to this goal.

Joshua R. Yates

Infrastructure

America's infrastructure, its roads, power plants and lines, bridges, dams, and other public goods, are in need of repair. Each year, reports illustrating the dire state of our nation's infrastructure remind us that if we continue to delay in replacing the worn out pieces of our infrastructure then we will end paying vastly more to replace them when they do finally suffer complete failure. However, if we are going to talk about infrastructure, then we should consider going deeper than just talking about roads, bridges, or public utilities. We should also talk about transportation – more importantly, personal vehicles and freight transportation that keep our nation going – as a whole.

Personal Transportation

Transportation (specifically our own personal transportation) is often an issue that people are adamant about. To say that someone should utilize public transportation rather than their own personal automobile is essentially telling someone that they should willingly give up their own personal set of wheels (a classic symbol of American freedom of movement), to ride the bus. For decades, having our own automobile (or SUV, Minivan, etc.) was more than just a dream; it was a coming of age moment for many Americans. We are unique among the world in the sheer number of personal vehicles we own, often one for every member of a household. The issue is not how many vehicles we own, nor that we want and demand the freedom of movement that having our own vehicle provides. Instead, what we need to consider is how we power our vehicles – the fuel, engines, and means by which the car is powered.

When we are talking about fuel, then we should address the principal fuel that most vehicles utilize, that being either gasoline or diesel. In our modern world, both of these fuels have rapidly increased in price and show no signs that this increase will abate any time in the near future. While gas prices may fluctuate, obviously what this trend means for all of us is that a greater share of our hard-earned income will be spent on fuel for our vehicles unless something changes. Additionally, there is the hidden cost of fuel price increases which also increases the cost of everything we buy, everything we eat, pretty much everything else in the economy given that the harvesting, manufacturing, and transportation of nearly everything we consume relies on fuel. Therefore, a portion (in some cases the bulk) of this fuel cost is passed on to consumers and added to the final price of what we buy. So, the real effect is that for as much as we feel the pain when we fuel up at the pump, we are also eating the extra costs in higher prices for everything else. That being said, we cannot simply blame oil companies or manufacturers/refiners, despite their record profits in the past decade. The issue instead is a lack of research and decisive action. At this critical juncture in our nation's history, we must take the decisive action to move beyond oil.

Joshua R. Yates

Moving Beyond Oil –
A 21st Century Strategy for Energy Independence

"What do we use other than oil?" I expect that you might be asking this question right now. Electric cars on the market today are either extremely expensive, extremely small, or both. They have extremely limited travel ranges and just aren't all that useful if you want to take a road trip or just go for a drive. Having to plug-in your car every few hours for a recharge does not make a trip fun or exciting, just slow and painful. Furthermore, what if you need to use air conditioning or a heater? With the batteries being drained for those "luxuries" how can electric cars even be remotely competitive with gasoline or diesel-powered cars? There are no electric trucks that are even on the horizon that can compete with current trucks in power and efficiency. "Hybrid" cars and trucks don't really get much better mileage than a regular engine and still cost too much more to buy. Betting that you will see the savings in fuel costs over time by paying more upfront for a supposedly more fuel efficient vehicle is just risky, and makes a lot of assumptions about future fuel costs that cannot be easily predicted. The truth is that what we do need is an electric engine that can do the job as well as an internal combustion engine, and for roughly the same cost in terms of price. That means, we need not just more research, but we also need real, actionable results.

Research for the sake of research is not useful, and fills too many academic journals that few people (outside of a small cadre of researchers) will ever read. Instead, what we need is research with the intention of achieving real solutions, not quick short-term fixes that will not make a real impact. What this means is that we need companies with capital (such as oil manufacturers) to partner with automobile manufacturers, and work together to develop batteries that can power a strong electric engine, can be charged rapidly, and work for a long duration. This is a major investment toward future profits for all of these companies, and a consortium effort on this would allow all of them to benefit from the technology. Sure, they could also sponsor research into this area, but that may or may not yield results, and would certainly not be as quick as focused research and development as a consortium by these companies. This research cannot take decades, cannot be treated as "blue sky" or ideas for some distant future. Our nation and our economy need solutions and results from American ingenuity now. This is essential to our position as a leader in this century, and to the continued strength of the American nation, economy, and people moving forward.

Perhaps I am being too hasty with respect to the speed by which I want to see this research occur, or how quickly I expect that results could realistically be achieved. However, I feel that the potential that exists from this research provides more than sufficient financial incentives for both our business community and the economy as a whole. Suppose if General Motors, Ford Motor Company, Exxon-Mobil, and ConocoPhillips, just to name a few, all cooperated on this research. Think of the sheer amount of resources that just these four companies could throw at this project in terms of capital, cash and materials. Sure, these are competitors in their respective industries, but they all benefit in the long run from cooperating at this juncture. Once the technology has been developed and proven, all of these companies and others as well, will find ways to improve the technology and to use it to suit their own business goals. There are times at which cooperation can produce a win-win situation for everyone. This is one of those times. The potential is there, it simply has to be realized.

We need more than just better batteries. We need stronger electric engines. We need to be able to achieve comparable power in a vehicle-sized electric engine that we see from existing combustion engines. If we are going to go full electric, then we need to be able to do the same job with an electric engine that one can do with any internal combustion engine, to and including heavy-duty work. More research is needed here as well. We cannot simply have stronger, better electric engines and have them relegated only to sub-compacts. I want to see trucks powered by these engines, from the smallest pickup trucks to the larger crew-cab-style work vehicles. I want to see freight trucks and construction equipment powered by electric engines. If we are going to truly step into the next century, it is time to think beyond gasoline, beyond diesel, and beyond oil.

One issue I have not yet addressed in this is refueling. If we are developing rapid-charge batteries, then we need to have the ability to recharge them as we travel. This is partly why I mentioned oil companies previously. Imagine if an incentive existed, such as a subsidy (short term, non-renewable, with a specific sunset date) to replace several pumps at existing stations with rapid recharge stations for these new vehicles. Eventually, the older internal combustion engines would phase out and all of the pumps would be replaced with recharge stations. This would allow existing facilities to be converted, rather than requiring new facilities and provide the means, through the short-term incentive, to make the change less demanding on these companies. By reducing the incentive to shift the cost of these renovations onto the consumer, life improves for all of us. If we already are used to "filling up" at a given station, why should we change that? We can continue to go there, switching from the old pump to the recharger instead.

The recharging units in these renewed stations would need to be developed simultaneously with the research for the new batteries. Not by the same researchers, of course, but separately at the same time as the battery research. That way, by the time the batteries are ready, we should have a working rapid recharge "pump" as well. If we develop these consecutively, rather than concurrently, we delay implementation of the entire new system. Results today does not mean delaying for another decade while we attempt to develop the other half of the new system that we need to power our vehicles and our society. I want results, not more delays and excuses, and to me consecutive development invites more delays and excuses as to why something cannot be done. America cannot afford more excuses or any more delays.

I have gone on for some time now about the need for electric cars, but let me be clear that this is not about "saving" the environment, or some hidden desire to save trees or the ozone layer or whatnot. No, this is simply about looking to the future. Simply put, there is a finite amount of oil in the world, regardless of how much that is or how long we project it to last. We cannot simply will more oil into being. When it runs out, it is gone. Given increasing global demand for oil, the cost of oil is increasing and our absolute reliance on oil (including as a fuel source) hurts our economy and our nation's position moving forward in this century. Rather than expect lower prices if some new supply of oil is found (especially since lower prices are unlikely to occur as long as additional profit can be made from reduced supply somewhere else in the production or delivery chain), we should make the needed technological developments to move beyond oil now. By doing so, we step ahead of the rest of the world, resume our place as the world's leader in technological development and remedy the stranglehold that oil has on the economy. Every technological shift that has occurred has left some companies obsolete. By paving the transition and helping to create the technology to move us forward, oil companies and other manufacturers remain technologically relevant, financially strong, and remain leaders in transportation and fuel in a post-oil world.

Joshua R. Yates

Railroads – Renewing America's Focus on Rail

During the 19th Century, one of our major innovations was to build railroads throughout America, with the goal being connection of one coast to another with a fast, efficient means of transportation. Sure, individuals could already cross the country with some form of road (dirt or otherwise) and had use of wagons and horses. However, we were thinking bigger than that and knew that the time to push forward was at hand. The same challenge faces us today. Rail, while it might seem a throwback to older technology, has come a long way from its origins. Modern rail networks are faster, safer, and more efficient than ever. They are also faster than ever. The cost is cheap, provided we renew our railway system with certain requirements in mind.

First, it is really improbable that every community throughout all of the United States would have a high speed rail connection, but every major city should have one. By major, I am using a definition that includes smaller cities, such as those with a population of 100,000 people. In some cases, there might be only one primary connection in a given state, but by including some smaller cities, we should be able to have greater connections in every state. There are many options to choose from when we look at high-speed rail, each with a different price point to consider and with different maintenance costs. Furthermore, given that some climates within the United States may be favorable to one type of high-speed rail as compared to another, we should consider the possibility that we utilize different high-speed rail equipment for different regions.

Second, the inclusion of more cities allows for more collection and drop-off points in the rail network, which is crucial to its success. In any fixed-rail system, inadequate collection or drop-off points doom the system to failure. This inadequacy could be that there are too many collection points or too many drop-off points, therefore some of these locations do not have the passenger load to sustain themselves. The issue is that we just do not know how many passengers might utilize a rail system until we begin construction and see it at work. Sure, there might be some cities which underperform in terms of passenger volume, but I suspect that these underperforming locations will be offset by other over-performing locations. Fares for the use of the train must be economical but cannot be subsidized by tax revenues to make it the only option people choose. Essentially, they should have choices: to purchase a car and pay for the vehicle, its maintenance, taxes, and so forth, take the train and pay the fare and potentially have to rent a car at your destination, or take an airplane and pay its fare while also potentially having to rent a car at your destination. The trade off should be a choice, but one that allows for individuals to make real comparisons between the three options. Sure, the airplane might be the only choice in some cases (overseas flights, for example) but if you want to go from Chicago to Dallas, any of the three can get you there; it just depends on how you want to go. Sure, highways will still be needed to get to a train station or an airport, but the choice still remains of not driving the entire distance to your final destination.

Third, the rail network must operate on a fixed time schedule. If the train is scheduled to depart at 4:45 p.m., then it absolutely should depart on-time. Any delays should be made immediately known through real-time monitoring, so passengers anywhere are aware of any delay. Real time updating of the location of the train would also be an essential element to add to every station, that way if a passenger is waiting for the arrival of the train, or family members awaiting the arrival of loved ones, can watch the train's progress. This same information should be available on-board the train as well. In addition, there should be enough trains available to have multiple trains running on routes where the volume is high enough to justify it.

Most important, though, is that these high speed rail lines must be able to operate at over 200 mph at all times, taking advantage of existing available property, such as alongside a highway, even if we built the rail line slightly elevated, preventing the removal of lanes from the existing highway. The shift from air travel to rail will bring our cities together in a way that we have not seen since the 19th century, with faster movement between cities and better-integrated regional markets. The question must be resolved, though, as to what we do with the existing rail lines if we are building a new high-speed rail network for passenger trains.

These existing rail lines should be upgraded and used solely as freight lines. They primarily function as freight lines in many locations now, so this might not seem all that different. However, when I suggest their use as freight lines, I am referring to both increased travel speeds (where possible), as well as the ability to carry heavier loads than at the present time. With the removal of all passenger trains from these lines, they should be able to function as the backbone of freight transportation within America. We need to encourage more freight to be moved by rail with the use of light trucks for local delivery, rather than freight transportation by highway. A revitalized railroad network will allow for a greater amount of freight to be removed from highways and other roads, reducing the maintenance costs (from damage due to weight on the road as a result of over-the-road freight) on our highways, and extending the life of these roads. The cost savings here will offset some of the costs associated with these rail improvements.

Air Travel

Air travel is not what it once was. I remember a time when going to the airport to see off or greet friends and family was a family affair. Everyone would go to the airport and wait by the gate with friends and loved ones before they boarded or waited together for you to arrive and disembark from the plane. Now, in the era of strip searches, x-ray scans, and groping by minimum-wage government drones, going to the airport is as about as enjoyable as having a surgery done by someone with no medical training, rusty equipment, and no anesthetic. That might be a bit of an exaggeration, yet there was a time when freedom of travel (without checkpoints, papers, and other harassment by the government in the name of security theater) in this country was acknowledged as a right. Part of our right to freedom of movement is a right not to be hassled and suspected as a criminal every time we travel, to not be asked "papers, please" within our country. Security theater, such as that at our airports, requires that one be viewed as a criminal outright, told that if we have nothing to hide then we should just comply without complaint. This kind of logic runs counter to everything we hold true in our country about freedom, but more importantly, that we view all citizens as innocent until proven guilty, not the reverse. Attempting to "stop" terrorists by forgetting what makes us American is the same as cutting off your nose to spite your face. It hands victory to terrorists and is frankly un-American.

With ever-increasing fares, offloading of fuel costs (and taxes on airlines) onto passengers, and revolving-door bankruptcy, air travel has shown that it is nearing the end of its lifespan. Furthermore, airlines and airports are perpetual money sinks. They are expensive to build, maintain, and operate. Aircraft are loud and costly to build. They use an inordinate amount of fuel, which consistently becomes increasingly more expensive to purchase. Air travel is increasingly expensive for passengers, with more of the costs being shifted to passengers in the form of fees and "taxes" for everything (luggage, boarding passes, security checkpoints and more). The goal becomes packing as many passengers as possible into a flying cattle car, not making the experience remotely enjoyable for the passengers. Overall, it is a consumer nightmare, one that we need to wean ourselves off.

Automobiles - Cars, Trucks and Freight

As I mentioned earlier, the quintessential image of American freedom of movement is the personal vehicle, whether it be a car, truck, minivan, SUV, or motorcycle. As Americans, we have a love/hate relationship with our vehicles. Our society and national landscape demand that nearly all of us own one (or more) vehicles to go to work, acquire groceries, visit entertainment venues, and so forth. All of these vehicles run on gasoline and/or diesel, both of which have become increasingly expensive over the past decade. I am sure that there are many of us that can remember when a gallon of gasoline was less than $1, and the anger that many of us had when gasoline began to climb over $1, $1.50, then $2, and so forth. Now, many of us stare at prices ranging from $3.50 to $5.00 a gallon. Some of this cost could be chalked up as inflation, but inflation has not been that meteoric over the past decade, and so that cannot account for the price increase. I won't debate the differing views on why price increases for gasoline or diesel at the pump or whom is to blame for it. This book is about solutions, not pointing fingers or assigning blame.

The real solution is not to insist that Americans drive less, or that we turn wholly to some form of mass transit or public transit system. Having lived in cities with public transit and those without it, it is really a non-starter. Sure, public transit (such as fixed-rail or subway systems) is nice to have when you have the right type of city for it, but many cities are just not designed to work with mass transit systems and are designed around highways instead. Busses do not always reach the destinations people want to go, and if they do, they are often too slow or too indirect. We want to move on our own terms and not be tied to when the bus finally gets arrives, either to pick us up or at our destination. As I mentioned, we have many cities that are simply highway towns. They are designed for highways, designed for personal vehicles, and to insist that they change to mass transit systems or other forms of public transportation would likely be cost-prohibitive and ultimately contradictory to their local cultural paradigm. The true solution is having cars and trucks that operate on a different fuel source. We need engines that do not rely on internal combustion for their source of power. What we need, as I mentioned earlier, are vehicles with true electric engines.

These new electric engines must be as powerful as our current gasoline or diesel powered engines. Currently, some fully electric vehicles do exist, and can be purchased. However, the battery life on all of these vehicles are simply too short, and the engines lack the power to tackle duties currently relegated to either gasoline or diesel engines. This is simply not good enough. If we are to make the transition from oil to power our vehicles and move forward to a new era in personal vehicles, then we need better batteries – batteries that not only last longer (going extremely long distances without a recharge) but provide enough power for an engine equally up to heavy-duty tasks (without rapidly draining the battery), and can be recharged rapidly at a station. The idea here is to maintain normalcy, even with the change in fuel. Your car (or truck) needs fuel, so you go to a station and "fill up;" however, instead of putting in gasoline, you hook up to a rapid recharger and pay for the electricity instead. This might seem like a pie-in-the-sky idea, but I truly believe that this is easily obtainable with modern technology. We, as Americans, have achieved great successes in our past. We have accomplished the impossible, and will always continue to do so. It is time for our next great leap forward in transportation, and that requires these new electric engines, capable of stepping up as a viable, real replacement, for internal combustion engines.

Why electric and not another fuel source, like ethanol, hydrogen, or fuel cells? The main reason is simple: ease of availability of fuel. Sure, we can make ethanol, but it burns faster than gasoline (you get less miles per gallon compared to gasoline) and uses corn, reducing food supplies and potentially raising the price of corn. Hydrogen is everywhere, but it is also highly combustible and I am unsure what might happen should two hydrogen-powered vehicles collide and the fuel tank be ruptured. If it were to explode, it might be more dangerous than our current fuel sources. However, hydrogen might be a viable option to supplement electric engines if we need one. It is easily available and can be liquefied for transport and use. I know that some companies are currently experimenting with hydrogen-powered vehicles, so this would be worth exploring further.

Fuel cells, as I understand it, are currently being experimented with as well by automobile manufacturers, but no vehicles utilizing the technology have been produced. However, if we continue research in this area, it might also be something to consider once an engine using fuel cells is shown to be at least as efficient (in fuel use) and powerful as a gasoline-powered (or diesel-powered) engine, at nearly identical cost. The shift away from oil is not, and cannot, be a path to higher prices simply as a means to end dependency on oil. It must be a new way forward, utilizing new technologies. Can some higher cost be absorbed if we are able to eliminate the fuel costs? Sure, but as with current hybrid vehicles, the increased cost for the vehicle cannot be so extreme that recovery of the cost as fuel cost savings is either negligible or impossible. With sufficient continued research, I would not discount either hydrogen or fuel cells as alternatives to gasoline. However, for the immediate future, the best choice is to focus on electric engines and the batteries to power them.

Infrastructure Repairs - Highways, Roads and Bridges

A drive on many highways throughout America nearly always reveals that our transportation infrastructure, namely roads, highways, and bridges, are in disrepair. We push maintenance into the future, hoping to get a little more out of our roads, before having to pay for (or actually do) repairs or replacement. Often, when maintenance is finally done, it is usually a patch, fill, or cover-up to try and hide the real problem: that many of our roads and bridges simply need to be completely replaced. The main question that I have asked many times is, where did the tax money go that was supposed to pay for these repairs? Do we not pay a tax every gallon of fuel (gasoline and diesel) that we buy, taxes that we are continually told are to be used for these repairs? Does the Federal government not allocate billions of dollars a year, even more of our tax money, for roads? Furthermore, why do our new roads, or even the recently repaired roads, fall apart so rapidly - is it perhaps shoddy construction, poor materials, or a lack of oversight? This is a question that our government should be able to answer as they spend billions of our tax dollars annually on roads that crumble as soon as they are completed.

However we want to look at it, we need to seriously revisit how the government, and by this I mean ALL government (local, county/parish, state, and federal) handle road construction and maintenance. Bridges should fall under the same level of scrutiny that should be applied to roads, so we can consider the two interchangeably. Road construction in many areas (generally speaking) is ridiculously slow. It is not uncommon in many places that I have visited to see construction equipment, signage, and cones out for years while construction takes place. Often, oddly, the equipment is idle for weeks, or even months, at a time. Worse cases are when a road sits partially completed, with work zone signage up (including cones) and no construction equipment in sight. Grass has grown over the entire worksite. Honestly, this is inexcusable. I am sure that if this was brought up to any number of officials they would say that road funding is done annually, and that construction only continues during the fiscal year, completing as much as is paid for in that fiscal year only.

What they are actually saying is that construction on the road will continue until the money runs out and then stop until the next batch of money is doled out for more construction. With funding done like this, it almost ensures that work will "continue" for years, and that by the time the work is finished some parts will be ready for new repair, keeping the cash-cow rolling. There is no reason to begin the road in one year, and finally complete it five, six, or ten years later. I cannot imagine constructing a building with the framing left openly exposed, with no further work done on the project, for a year before I bothered to attach the roof or put up walls, then in the third year to put in windows and doors, only to complete the building in the fourth or fifth year. It is ridiculous that this is how we construct public roads in America.

The first step in a solution must be reform with how we pay for road construction. Rather than the piecemeal payment schedule that we currently use, we really should either pay upfront in full, or pay in two or three payments. One third upfront, one third at the midpoint, and the final third upon completion according to quality inspection and plan specifications. Failure to observe proper quality control at any point in the project and penalties could be imposed, to and including loss of the contract due to breach of contract on the part of the construction firm. Whether we pay all at once or in a structured payment schedule of two or three payments, the point remains that the piecemeal allocations to road construction which drag out the process over several years must end.

What we also need is oversight. Simply because the road is finished does not mean it is what we paid for. The specifics should be, and likely are, clear in the contracts signed when the road construction begins. What we need is follow up. If the agreement was for materials and construction that should last for 20 years (preferably more), then if the road is failing (at all) within one year (or even ten years), that is a breach of contract. This does not mean that the company goes out and simply puts down a patch or fills a hole. No, there should be repercussions for those companies that do shoddy work or perform construction that fails to do what was promised when they received the contract. This is not difficult: do the work, do it right the first time, get paid.

The problem is that without some sort of built-in ramifications for breach of contract due to negligence or poor work on the part of the contractor, it is likely that the solution they would offer would involve slicing the individual road section out and replacing it or simply patching over it. So, what we end up with is an obstacle course of potholes and patches (which cost extra money that we are also paying) instead of the quality road that we originally paid for. Sure, I expect some level of decay on any structure or road that we build, but having worked with concrete previously, I can tell you with certainty that the amount of maintenance and repairs that I see on roads when I travel tells me that quality controls are either critically insufficient or are being completely being ignored. Quality concrete construction, when done right, lasts for decades with minimal repairs, even under heavy use. It is, truly, the permanent solution. Concrete that has holes, cracks, and starts to crumble within one or two years (or less) is not quality, and it shows. We wouldn't need to have roads constantly repaired if they would have been built right the first time. What is to stop that bridge from falling out from underneath you when you drive across it? It does happen. In nearly every case, shoddy construction, poor quality materials, or a lack of proper maintenance are to blame.

Road construction done right lasts for decades, and does not cost more money. In all honesty, quality construction (done right the first time) costs less money than shoddy construction which is constantly being repaired. It simply requires our government to inspect and continually verify that the construction is proceeding as planned, quality is being maintained (and no shortcuts are being made on any step of the process, which should be considered a likely possibility given that government universally grants construction contracts to the lowest bidder), and that projects are being done on budget and on time, not sitting idle for years in various stages of completion.

Aside from simply adding oversight, however, there are real funding issues with our infrastructure. We have a lot of roads, bridges, and highways now, more than ever before in our nation's history, with new roads being constructed at this very moment. These roads will require maintenance and as such we must turn our attention to how we pay for these roads and bridges given that we should be spending money to establish faster transportation options, such as a new high-speed rail network. I am sure some of you might be asking, "If we're spending money on trains then where do we get it for roads?" Oversight on projects is one area that we can experience a cost savings, although it is not upfront. The savings is realized, for example, through reduction (and elimination) of double spending on projects by paying for construction and then paying for repairs.

Build it right the first time, and we don't waste money on repairs.

To further remedy the issue of infrastructure decay, we also need to focus on two areas: road usage and infrastructure bonds. Road usage is simply measuring the amount of load that a road actually carries over a period of time. Why measure road usage? If we know how many, or how heavy, vehicles are that use specific roads and highways, and the frequency of their use, it will help to gauge whether or not new roads are needed or how much maintenance is expected on the current roads in that particular location at the present time. By anticipating needed repairs, replacements, and upgrades, we as a nation will be better poised to handle tomorrow's infrastructure needs. That brings us to the second area of focus: infrastructure bonds.

Infrastructure Bonds - Invest in America

Infrastructure bonds, simply put, are an investment in America. These bonds would provide funding directly for infrastructure improvements in our country, be it roads, bridges, railroad construction, electric power lines, or broadband access expansion, or maintenance on any of these as well, as examples. These funds would be restricted only to use on infrastructure projects, and could not be used to fund anything else. No I.O.U. receipts as is done with Social Security funds. These dollars would not be convertible for use in the general revenue pool, that way you would know that every dollar you invest in infrastructure bonds goes directly to what you intended. Infrastructure bonds are, finally, a means for our nation to repair, upgrade, and advance our internal infrastructure without cutting from essential functions, such as defense. Even more, it is a way for private citizens to finally have more direct control over government spending. Rather than relying on politicians in our state capitols or in Washington, D.C. to solve the issue, we would have a mechanism to solve it ourselves. It is not a total solution, not yet, but would provide a means to get us there.

As a nation, without a strong and well-maintained infrastructure, we are destined to drive on crumbling roads, watch as dams and levees fail, witness more bridges collapsing, and continue the blackouts and brownouts of recent years. Our nation would continue its slide backwards and we would be no longer the world's leader, but just another second or third-rate nation. That just is not where America should be. We have been a world leader for more than a century, and our leadership is needed now more than ever. We need infrastructure investment now. Investments that will create new jobs, update our decades-old infrastructure, and lay the foundation for a renewed 21st century America.

Infrastructure bonds would be, by their very nature, government bonds, each with a 20-year maturity rate. Annually, the bonds would accrue interest at a rate of 3.471%. This would result in a $1,000 bond being worth $2,000 once it matures. At an annual interest rate of 3.471%, the infrastructure bonds would easily beat out nearly every interest-bearing savings or checking account available nationally today and would beat the interest rates on virtually all CDs (Certificates of Deposit) available at the present time as well. It is, quite frankly, a solid (and safe) investment. Simply put, once purchased, the face value of an infrastructure bond doubles upon maturity, similar to U.S. Savings Bonds available today. After the bond matures, you have two choices. You can cash it out, and take the full cash value of the bond (with no taxes on these funds, ever), or you can roll over the bond, using the current value of the bond to purchase a new bond for another 20 years. If this is confusing, allow me to illustrate with an example.

Suppose you decided to buy an infrastructure bond in 2015 in the amount of $1,000. Twenty years pass, and the amount of interest accrued has left the bond that you purchased for $1,000 now worth $2,000. You can choose to take the $2,000 in cash, with no taxes on this money, or you can turn your $2,000 around and use it to buy another infrastructure bond, for another 20 years, anticipating a value of $4,000 at its maturity. Your entire investment was $1,000 and after 40 years you walk away with $4,000. Sure, it is a long time to wait, but you do retain the option of cashing the bond out at any point in the 20 years, provided you are willing to accept less total interest accrued as a mild penalty for cashing the bond out early. If you cashed out the bond within the first five years, you would be assessed a penalty which eliminates any interest you have accrued to that point. You always retain the original face value of the bond at purchase, so any penalty would never reduce you below that initial amount. These are long-term investments to benefit our country, and as such, the returns are worth it, the risk is virtually nonexistent, and the penalties for early withdrawal are fair. Besides, what is a more guaranteed investment strategy than investing in a road that you will drive on for 20 years to work, or the bridge you drive on to cross the river, especially knowing that after 20 years, you doubled your money without having to do anything other than live your life in our great nation?

I cannot talk highly enough of the idea of infrastructure bonds. This is a means by which we can ensure that our money is going to a specific set of projects, rather than to other areas of our government. Furthermore, as revenue for infrastructure bonds increases, that is money we can stop spending from tax revenue on infrastructure. That means national debt retirement (elimination), it means eliminating deficits, and it means balanced budgets and lower taxes. Not all at once, of course, but over time these can all be realized as we restore fiscal responsibility throughout our government at all levels.

Energy Production

Another component of our infrastructure is our nation's electric power grid. More than simply transmission lines, the power grid is comprised of our electric power facilities as well, such as power plants. Looking forward at the future, we should take a closer look at the ways in which we generate electric power for our homes, our businesses, and potentially, our transportation as well. If, for example, we are going to rely on vehicles that operate on electric power, rather than gasoline, we need a power network that can handle the extra load, which may require new, additional facilities to be constructed and for older facilities to be upgraded or replaced.

Coal - The Traditional Power Source

Coal has been a component of power production throughout the world since the industrial revolution and is still a primary means of energy production today. Very little has changed about the concept that drives electric production by use of coal other than the technology that we use to create that power. First, we should be specific when we talk about "coal." Coal, used generally, is the name given to four different types of the same resource: anthracite, bituminous, subbituminous, and lignite. These four, listed in order of highest energy content to lowest, are all available in the United States. However, if we were to talk about the greatest quantity that the United States has available, bituminous surpasses the others in terms of sheer amount of reserves, followed by anthracite coal. Beyond energy content, the four listed are also in order of cleanest burning to dirtiest burning coal. If we had the option, anthracite coal would be the go-to choice. It burns the cleanest and provides the highest amount of energy. However, anthracite coal is more expensive, and thus many utilities use bituminous coal instead due both its greater availability of supplies and lower price. If these utility providers were to use the more expensive (and more efficient) anthracite coal, they would need to pass that on to the customers, in part at least, and that would mean higher utility rates. With current technology, such as scrubbers, we can easily make turn bituminous coal into a safe, clean, entirely domestic fuel source to power America in the 21st century.

So why are we discussing different types of coal? To put it simply, coal is absolutely a 100% domestic power source that we have in very large quantities here in the United States. Coal power means more jobs here in America, a break from reliance on foreign fuel sources, and a path to true energy independence. To keep our domestic coal flowing to our power plants, we must re-

Mining safety is crucial, to prevent mine collapses such as the one recently in West Virginia, as well as preventing mine fires, such as the several that have been burning for decades in Pennsylvania. Furthermore, we must protect the long-term health of our miners, lest they develop conditions such as "black lung" which is entirely preventable.

member that we need to take care of one of our most crucial assets: our miners. Our mines and the miners that work within them are a national resource, one that we must protect if we are to continue relying on coal as a 100% domestic fuel source. With coal, we have no need to rely on other countries for fuel, we do not need to be concerned with hostilities in locations halfway around the world, nor do we have need to be concerned with closures of ocean thoroughfares for its delivery. With electric vehicles, powered by energy created from 100% domestic coal, we can absolutely end our reliance on foreign oil imports and finally achieve true American energy independence in this century. We should focus on growth through coal, putting our energy policy on the right track; stable an independent. Safe, strong, productive mines are needed; protecting our environment, our miners, and our future by freeing our nation's economic growth from the whims of the global fuel market.

One argument that I hear often when I discuss coal power is that coal power generation is inherently dirty and therefore we should turn to non-polluting power sources, such as wind and solar. While I am not opposed to looking at wind and solar, which I will discuss shortly, I admit that I am an ardent supporter of coal power. Coal power production does not need to be inherently dirty power. In fact, technology exists today to "scrub" emissions, thus reduce the harmful emissions from our coal plants. The one caveat is that is it currently expensive to retrofit coal plants with the new technology and equally as expensive to build a new plant with the scrubbers in place from day one. There is, however, a compromise solution. If we focus on coal production as the primary means of electric power generation for the foreseeable future, then we must acknowledge that we will need to utilize some "dirty" coal plants for the short run, retrofitting these plants later to add the emissions scrubbers. Coal plants operate for many decades, and so if we focus on adding scrubbers in the first ten or fifteen years (on new plants), then we would still have full operational capacity at the plant for 35 or 40 years with the scrubbers in-place.

However, the issue remains of how to pay for the scrubbers themselves. With the use of infrastructure bonds, the cost to add the scrubbers would be covered. Want cleaner coal plants? Buy infrastructure bonds! Entirely new clean coal plants could be built through infrastructure bond monies, but this should be secondary to the primary goal of improving, advancing, and re-pairing our existing infrastructure, including our existing coal power plants with improvements such as emissions scrubbers.

Nuclear Power - The Modern Alternative

Mention nuclear power, and the mere idea is usually followed with one of three thoughts: disaster, meltdown, and radiation. Nuclear power disasters such as Chernobyl and Three Mile Island are often mixed with recent images of the disaster at the Fukushima Dai-ichi reactor in Japan. What we need to realize is that these disasters are completely isolated incidents. There are many nuclear power stations that are operating right this minute, worldwide, which have never experienced any error or failure ever. We must remember these disasters, terrible as they are, are the anomaly and are not the norm. Nuclear power today is not the bogeyman that we were once, and often still are, told that it is. Nuclear power is safe power. Meltdowns and accidents are so rare that statistically you stand a greater chance of being in an airplane crash today than of experiencing a nuclear disaster at any point in your life. Modern nuclear reactors are 100% clean (which is to say that they produce no emissions, not that they produce no waste), and with current techniques for fuel reclamation and waste storage, nuclear power can provide a bridge to the future.

Our nation's military, particularly the Navy, has safely utilized nuclear power for decades. The many nuclear power plants within our country have operated safely for decades. There are many other countries throughout the world safely utilizing nuclear power today. Many of our plants are decades old, and newer plants constructed around the world today take advantage of new technologies which are safer and more efficient than ever. Nuclear power is the safest, cleanest, and cheapest source of power available. Nuclear power can, and should be a primary power source for our electric power grid, operating along with our coal plants, to provide the security and safety that our nation requires of its electric production network, paving the way forward into the 21st century.

Solar, Wind and Geothermal - The Natural Alternatives

When we talk about clean energy, aside from nuclear or clean coal power, what we're really talking about are three forms of power generation: solar, wind, and geothermal. In many cases, these forms of electric power generation are simply not economically feasible for mass energy production at this point in their development. If you are in a location which has long periods of darkness, frequent storms, heavy snow, ice, or hail, then solar panels are likely not the chief way in which you'll be generating electric power. Solar power might provide supplemental electricity, and that is fantastic, but it cannot be relied upon as an effective means to generate large quantities of electricity during periods of time where it cannot harness sunlight. You would still need some other form of electric power generation, such as coal or nuclear power, to handle the situations where solar panels are producing insufficient electricity to meet demand at that time. Solar power is good technology, and we should continue developing it as a key component of our future energy strategy. It cannot, however, be the only component or our primary focus as a means of national electric power generation at this time.

Construction of solar power generation facilities require a large open area exposed to sunlight for extremely long periods of time where the solar panels and reflective mirrors can concentrate the light. This works well in areas such as the southwestern United States, where these conditions often exist. However, solar power is less feasible where either the space is not there to construct a large solar facility, or due to other geographic constraints, such as in a mountainous region, hurricane prone region, or tornado prone region. This does not however preclude people (or businesses) in these regions from placing solar panels on the roofs of their buildings or homes. In fact, this supplemental energy production reduces the load on electric facilities during summer months when many of us operate air-conditioners. During the evening hours, more traditional electric power plants would still be the primary means of powering our homes and businesses. Perhaps, in the future, given the rapid developments in technology, solar power will be feasible as a primary means of power generation for portions of our energy grid. We should encourage this technology, as it provides energy with no emissions; no additional fuel sources, and produces no waste. All it requires is access to the sun.

Wind power is the second natural alternative for electric power generation. Like solar power, wind power has particular constraints as to which regions it is optimally suited for. Large scale electric production from wind requires vast numbers of wind towers, just a mass energy production through solar power requires vast numbers of solar panels. These towers, collectively, require a great deal of geographic space to adequately produce a sufficient amount of electric power for a small community or a city. In some regions, such as larger cities, where land is at a premium or transition of land to large scale wind or solar power is an impossibility, this is just not feasible. However, as with solar, individual wind towers can provide supplemental electric power to individual businesses and homes, even if they cannot power the entire community. A home or business which has both solar panels and wind towers as supplemental forms of power generation could save a great deal of money in the long run and reduce their reliance on the local power facilities, even transferring the excess power generated back to the utility for use elsewhere (in exchange for a credit against their bill). Compensation for this excess power would reduce the overall electric expenses for individuals and businesses. This is a win for individuals, business, and for utility companies.

Geothermal power is a term that I use generally for all forms of power that rely on heat from the earth or from water (such as hydroelectric power). Technically speaking, hydroelectric power could have its own separate section, but for ease of reference here I consider it alongside traditional geothermal power. Why combine the two? Both forms of power, traditional geothermal and hydroelectric, rely on sources of power that derive from earthbound natural resources (such as rivers or thermal vents). For hydroelectric power, for example, unless you are near a river that you can effectively dam (including accounting for all of the damage such a dam will cause to the surrounding region and downriver, for example), this is not an option for your area. Traditional geothermal power is also extremely expensive, in terms of initial capital outlay, similar to constructing a hydroelectric dam.

For these reasons, I cannot recommend geothermal power as a primary means of electric power generation in our power grid. It is useful in regions where it exists, but is less likely to be feasible for large scale production outside of existing dams any time in the near future. We cannot simply dam every river in America for power generation. It would forever alter the fabric of our nation, our landscape, and the regions which rely on our rivers for their livelihood. Geothermal power, sadly, is just not the direction that our nation needs to go. We need power sources that can be feasible for large regions of our country, we need solar and wind power as auxiliary power sources to our primarily coal and nuclear powered energy grid.

We've already talked a bit about the need to upgrade our electric power grid, focusing primarily on power plants. However, another area that we must look at is the power lines themselves. Electric power is bought and sold daily on the open market, which means, depending on where you live and if your local utility is buying power on the market, your electricity might have been produced at a distant power plant and sold to your local utility. The problem here is not that we do not have a sufficient number of electric lines to move excess power around the nation. It is that we need newer, more efficient power lines that lose less power during the transmission process. If your utility has to buy power from elsewhere to power your home or business, they are paying for more power than they will actually get, due to having to factor in transmission loss. That translates to higher costs to you, the consumer. Less power lost during transmission from the point where it is generated (power plant or facility) to where it is used (your home or business) means lower costs for all electricity and that means savings in your pocket. In addition, we need redundancy in these lines in case of a line failure or other event, therefore allowing the load to be switched to a different line as needed to prevent blackouts or brownouts. This would be similar to the primary and secondary power plants we discussed previously.

Beyond simple convenience, there is a security benefit to be gained from this sort of redundancy. Should a natural disaster (such as a hurricane, tornado, or earthquake) or a terrorist (foreign or domestic) destroy one particular set of power lines (or a substation or power plant), our nation's utility providers would have the means to quickly and easily shift the load and restore power. There would have to be serious, catastrophic damage to the power grid at a significant number of locations to actually cripple this flexible, redundant network and as a result cause more than a momentary inconvenience. Even committing an act of terrorism involving a power plant itself would prove moot at causing electric interruption on a large scale. Other power plants, located elsewhere, could pick up the demand in short order, restoring power easily to those affected without any major additional effort anywhere in the power grid. We cannot discount the need to strengthen and upgrade out power lines when we are discussing our overall infrastructure needs.

Internet Access - A 21st Century Utility

Let's be honest - in today's world, having access to broadband Internet is not a luxury, it is a necessity. As such, access to broadband Internet should be treated as a public good, similar to a road or electricity. Unfortunately, access to broadband Internet service has not received the same level of attention as a vital component of our infrastructure. Instead, broadband Internet access is viewed by many as a luxury, even as access to government, many businesses, schools, and libraries is shifted online to the Internet. While other nations around the world have high-speed Internet available for all of their citizens, we have a disjointed network of different Internet providers with a plethora of different speeds, nearly all of them slow or throttled (reducing your speed based on usage). The fact that we still have individuals connecting to the Internet with dial-up modems shows that we have simply failed in our task of bringing this nation entirely into the current century.

There was a time that I, like some of you, connected to bulletin boards (BBS services) with a dial-up modem. Remember baud rates and nodes? What about text browsers (such as Lynx)? How about DOS, OS/2, or Windows 3.1? 5.25" or 3.5" floppy disks, monochrome monitors, and booting from a floppy (prior to hard drives) or using tapes for storage might be unheard of for many young Americans, but it was this technology that paved the way for today's smartphones and tablet computers. The point is that it is thought by some that this is technology that has come and gone, except that it hasn't. Instead of providing this broadband Internet access for everyone through public utilities, we have been taught to believe that broadband Internet access is only for those people who can afford it, and the rest of us should make do without it. As businesses and government shift access online and social media continues to integrate our society and how we interact, the need for high-speed Internet for everyone becomes paramount. At that point, it becomes a public good.

Let's be clear what I mean by "high-speed" when I reference Internet speed. I do not mean the almost universally misleading (nigh deceptive) "up to" some speed, such as 10Mbps, which is commonly mistaken to mean 10 megabytes per second. Without getting overly technical, let's be clear what this truly means. 10Mbps is 10 megabits (Mb) per second, with is roughly 1.2 megabytes (MB) per second. Notice the difference between Mb and MB? The capitalization of the B is key here. This distinction is never stated in any of the advertising. We are told only that speeds may vary (and they do), and that in some cases customers may not achieve the "highest" speeds. What I mean by "high-speed" is Internet access that exceeds 1Gbps, or one gigabit per second. To put this into perspective, your 56k dial-up modem transfers data at a rate of 56 kilobits per second (Kbps), or 56,000 bits per second. A megabit, the next step up in speed, is 1000 Kbps. A gigabit, by comparison, is 1,000,000 Kbps, or 1000 megabits per second (Mbps). We have the technology to achieve gigabit speeds for our broadband access, what we lack is the political will throughout our government to make broadband Internet (true high-speed Internet) a public good. We pride ourselves on being a technologically advanced world leader, yet our Internet access is still largely stuck in the late 20th century. To truly enter this century, we need Internet access befitting a first-class nation; we need nothing less than the best.

This does not mean that we should commoditize Internet access further and only those with the financial means get access while the rest of us common folk are relegated to technology straight out of 1990 or 2000. This merely illustrates even more why we need to make Internet access a public utility. Utilities have the power, through economies of scale, to effectively make the investment necessary to upgrade and support a data network of this size and speed, even if it means co-opting or contracting with private enterprise to accomplish this. Therefore, when a building is wired for electric power access, the utility company can connect the building's Internet access at the same time, along with any other utility connections that might be in order. The customer is ready to on day one. Simple, cost effective, and long overdue. Internet access is as vital to our society as electricity and running water. It is time that we made it as much of a priority as other infrastructure needs.

A New Vision for America:

A Call to Action

Let's be forthright about this – it's time we, as Americans, got off our collective rear-ends and did something about the problems facing our beloved nation. I know we are all busy – especially in this economy. But it is one thing to complain about the state of our country and the ills of our society. It is a totally different ball game – and admittedly, more work – to actually do something about it. Too many times we may think "it won't matter if I vote, so why do it?"

Throughout this book, I have spent a great deal of time discussing some of the challenges currently facing our nation and presented solutions to those challenges that we can make a reality today. However, the most important element in making any changes in our country lies within all of us. The greatest key to any reform in our government, at every level, is in actions that we take as citizens.

There are several things that we can do, right now, wherever we are, and I challenge you to take the first steps with me today to put America first, to become informed, to vote, and to get involved.

Get Involved Locally

The greatest impact that we can achieve always starts locally. By being involved, your voice will be heard more clearly than by simply voting. Do you know when your local city council meets and where? Attend a meeting! Ask questions and hold those elected officials accountable. Many localities have other government panels whose meetings are open to the public, such as zoning or utilities boards. Find where they meet and when and go to a meeting. Furthermore, don't just go to these meetings. Get involved in your neighborhood and community in other ways. Form a neighborhood watch or a neighborhood committee to put into action the changes that need to be made. Get to know your neighbors. Talk about the challenges that are facing your local community and then use that dialogue to work with each other to find real solutions to those challenges. Frankly, it needs to start with talking to one another. Whether as neighbors, coworkers, or citizens, we simply don't talk to each other anymore. We talk past one another, or at one another. We automatically treat each other with suspicion. We must listen to one another again, not simply talk to hear ourselves speak. We must stop assuming everyone is out to get us, or that they are simply waiting for the right moment before they do something to hurt us. At our core, we're just decent people. We need to remember that and work civilly to solve the problems our communities face.

At the same time, we can all find numerous things that might be local challenges, but finding and implementing solutions is what we need to focus on. Find an issue that needs resolution from your local government. Bring that issue up at a meeting, presenting both the issue and your proposed solution. Are you the person that everyone turns to with concerns? Consider running for city council (or the board of aldermen in some communities) and work to ensure that your community's needs are met while keeping the rest of the local government accountable and responsible.

Scrutinizing your local community and its government are both extremely important, but that does not mean that our state and federal governments do not also deserve the same level of scrutiny. We need individuals to step forward and run in primary elections to take back control of government at all levels. If we, as a people – a collective citizenry – want to keep our government fiscally conservative, then we must acknowledge that both political parties have contributed to the gross overspending and poor tax policy of our government, especially at the federal level (but also in many states and municipalities). We need true fiscal conservatives who understand that every dollar that is taken from us in taxes or fees is a dollar that we cannot spend on our families. The same focus on community that we seek at the local level can and must be applied to our statehouses and in the federal government.

VOTE!

Vernon Dahmer, an American civil rights leader, once said "If you don't vote, you don't count." I would go further, and say that not only do you not count if you do not vote, but that you forfeit the right to complain about your government, taxes, or any trampling on your other rights and liberties. That may sound harsh, but we must remember that the right to vote is one of our most sacred rights in the United States. Sure, we might argue about Voter ID laws or other measures, which some have called attempts at voter suppression. However, the fact remains that if you do not actively stand up and exercise your right to vote, or even attempt to do so, then your views simply do not count. You have willingly surrendered your most potent weapon and said that you are alright with a small minority dictating to you what you can and cannot do. You have given your implied consent to that same group to take your money, your property, and your freedoms at will. Your vote, even if you vote for the losing candidate or on the losing side of a resolution, counts. It always counts. If you refuse to exercise the right to vote simply because you think your candidate might lose then you have created a self-fulfilling prophesy. Who knows how many other people thought the same thing, and if you all had voted, your candidate might actually have won. Our vote is our voice; it is our single most powerful weapon. Do not let anyone take that from you. Men and women, coming to America from many different countries and of many races and religions have fought and died so that you can have that right to vote. Do not dishonor their actions by refusing to exercise it. Stand up and vote. Make the time. It is THAT important.

Be Informed!

When you go to vote, and you SHOULD be voting, ensure that you are fully informed! However harsh it may sound, too many people tend to 'vote stupid.' There is an ever-increasing amount of political campaign advertising and spending from candidates and outside groups blasting deliberate "misinformation" through television, radio, and over the Internet at us constantly. Don't let these advertisements be the only way you get information before you vote. Challenge yourself to get informed on just a few issues at a time, maybe one or two, then look those up, see how these might affect you and your family and friends. Make your decision based on that, rather than based on advertisements, misconstrued remarks, or talking points from anyone, politician, news anchor, or otherwise. Inform yourself on the issues, and then vote based on that knowledge. Simply put, trust yourself and what you know or learn about an issue, a proposed law, or a candidate. Don't merely trust what an ad or some news show tells you about your fellow Americans who are running for elected office. Even more, don't make your decision based on a poll. You have to decide what is best for you and yours, not what is best because a pollster said it was popular. Just because something is popular, or unpopular, does not make it right or wrong. It just makes it popular or unpopular. Prohibition was popular for a time, but that did not make it right. It just made a colossal mess that required another constitutional amendment to undo. You have the right to be informed before you vote. Exercise that right. Remember, we are the government ("We the People") and we have the power over our government, not the other way around.

America FIRST!

We need a shift in our entire national conversation to one which truly puts America first. Instead of focusing on internal issues in other countries, or constantly projecting power around the world, we have very real issues right here at home that we need to address. From runaway federal spending, to perpetual wars, to chronic unemployment and continual recession, we have no shortage of issues we need to address right here at home. Around the world, if you ask individuals in other countries which they place first, their own country or some other country around the world, I can guarantee you that the answer will be their own country comes first, above all else.

Even with globalization in our business world, nationalism remains. I want to see politicians here in the United States, for example, who are willing to stand up and make the hard choices, placing the needs of our country first, rather than any ally or other country we are providing "aid" to. If we cannot afford to take care of our own people, then we have no business sending money for ANY REASON to another country. Other countries are not sending cash here to help us with our internal issues. The era of the United States being the world's perpetual cash machine has to end. We cannot be the global enforcer, nor can we pass around money that we do not have to give. America FIRST, I say. Looking inward and focusing on our issues does not make us isolationist, nor does it mean that we are not looking around the world at issues that might occur. It does not mean that we have disengaged from the world. It simply means that we are looking to our own needs first, and then we can look at improving conditions elsewhere. We cannot be the example to the world if our cities are bankrupt, our infrastructure is crumbling, our nation is unemployed, and we have no money left because we have a populace that is so impoverished that tax revenue plummets. At that point, we are regressing backwards as a country and that is not something that any of us should ever accept.

A strong America requires that we place America FIRST in every thought, every word, and every deed of our government. No more offshoring, outsourcing, or placing foreign interests ahead of our own. We cannot assume that because we stop paying the bills for countries around the world that they will somehow not be able to support themselves. What it will do is force them to rethink their own expenditures and to determine for themselves what their priorities are, just as we must do for ourselves.

While we are placing America first, we must also keep in mind that no matter how big a problem may seem, or how complex it may appear, that there is nothing that we cannot overcome or achieve together. Americans throughout history have overcome challenges that others thought insurmountable. We have achieved fantastic things, and will continue to do so. Working together, Americans can achieve anything that we set our minds, our hands, and our wills toward. Stand up with me and let's make this century the best century in the history of the United States of America! Let us work to create a future for ourselves, our children, and their children that will ensure America not only continues to survive but thrives as a bastion of opportunity, freedom, and liberty for centuries to come.

About the Author

Joshua R. Yates is a political strategy, policy design and implementation consultant, and a historian, with advanced study in United States and Japanese history, political science, economics and economic history, and communication/ rhetoric. He lives and works near Springfield, Missouri.

He currently works as executive director for New Manifest Destiny and as a partner in the consulting firm, Yates & Associates. The firm provides expertise to the nonprofit, government agency, and small business sectors. Services include policy design and analysis, efficiency improvement and business development, fundraising, public relations, nonprofit management, leadership and management development, webinars, workshops, and training.

Mr. Yates is available as both a speaker and for political and policy consultations. He can be easily reached online through email at jyates@newmanifestdestiny.com. You can follow him on Twitter at http://twitter/com/newmanifestdest.